Parker Palmer is one of our wisest minds and lives and one of my greatest mentors. He has the spirit of a poet and the stature of a prophet. There is no one I'd rather eavesdrop on as he ponders "the brink of everything." This book is a companion for not merely surviving a fractured world, but embodying—like Parker—the fiercely honest and gracious wholeness that is ours to claim at every stage of life.

—**KRISTA TIPPETT,** founder of On Being Studios, author of *Einstein's God* and *Becoming Wise,* winner of the 2014 National Humanities Medal

Parker Palmer is the most integral and wholehearted teacher of our age. For nearly eight decades, he has seen much, questioned everything, and returned with a wisdom essential to everyone. His latest book, *On the Brink of Everything,* is a deep reflection on aging that offers a master's earned view of the large and the small, and how we're all vital threads woven together by life. This book will stir your soul and bring you closer to everything.

—**MARK NEPO,** author of *More Together Than Alone* and *The Book of Awakening*

Parker J. Palmer's tenth wise book, *On the Brink of Everything,* is a wondrously rich mix of reality and possibility, comfort and story, helpful counsel and poetry, in the voice of a friend. It's an honest wake-up chime, no matter where you are in your own time line, because somehow, these pages hold all of time—past and present, stirring together—refreshing the spirit. This is a book of immense gratitude, consolation, and praise.

—**NAOMI SHIHAB NYE,** author of *Transfer* and *Voices in the Air: Poems for Listeners*, and National Book Award finalist

Our entire culture is deeply in need of true elders, and you can't be one until you have arrived there—chronologically, spiritually, and intellectually. Parker J. Palmer is a writer and a man who has clearly earned the title of elder. And he elders with such readability and humor! This book is a generous gift to all of us—and to our attempts at a truly human civilization.

—**RICHARD ROHR,** founder of the Center for Contemplation and Action, and author of *Falling Upward* and *Adam's Return*

Parker J. Palmer's books are long-treasured companions on my personal journey. His newest offering is clear-eyed and good-humored, luminously prophetic and disarmingly honest. It is tender to the core for our shared human condition and fierce with love and unguarded hope for our shared human possibility. It has the feel of a lovely kitchen table conversation between the author and reader, exploring thoughtful aging, finding meaning in hard times, and harmonizing our inner and outer landscapes at every stage of life. This book is a generous gift to a worried and weary world.

—**CARRIE NEWCOMER,** musician, recording artist of *The Beautiful Not Yet*, author of *A Permeable Life: Poems and Essays*, and Grammy songwriting award winner

Parker Palmer has given me so many gifts through the years. His writing has done for me what I can only hope mine does for others. *On the Brink of Everything* has given me new and special gifts. Parker, now in his late seventies, has helped this guy in his early sixties think of my years ahead as "triple wrapped in mystery." Savoring this book is a kind of mentorship in aging, and it ends in a crescendo of poetry. My first thought when I turned the last page: "I want to read this again from the beginning, starting right now."

—**BRIAN D. McLAREN**, author of *The Great Spiritual Migration*

Parker Palmer has been a mentor and midwife to countless young people in my generation, including me. When I was in my twenties standing at a crossroads, his book *Let Your Life Speak* inspired me to pursue an untraditional path as an activist-artist; he released the music within me. Now in my thirties, as the cacophony of vitriol and violence becomes deafening, his friendship teaches me how to remain faithful to my own melodies and keep playing them. In the darkness, Parker has taught me how to wonder at the night sky, keep death in my mind's eye, and listen to the wisdom of my grandfather and ancestors, whose music lives within mine. He has poured these insights into a book that feels more like a treasure chest. *On the Brink of Everything* is filled with gems of wisdom, each a prism that helps us see our own vast interiority and sing our own truths. My greatest aspiration is to journey through life and arrive at the brink as Parker has, with humility and faithfulness, and pockets full of gems.

—**VALARIE KAUR**, civil rights activist, lawyer, filmmaker, and founder of the Revolutionary Love Project

One of the wisest people on the planet has written one of the finest books on growing b/old gracefully. This warm and witty book will delight and inspire readers of all ages.

—**RICHARD LEIDER,** best-selling author or coauthor of *The Power of Purpose, Repacking Your Bags,* and *Life Reimagined*

ON the BRINK
of EVERYTHING

Other Books by Parker Palmer

The Active Life

The Company of Strangers

The Courage to Teach

Healing the Heart of Democracy

The Heart of Higher Education (with Arthur Zajonc)

A Hidden Wholeness

Let Your Life Speak

The Promise of Paradox

To Know as We Are Known

ON the BRINK
of EVERYTHING

Grace, Gravity, and Getting Old

PARKER J. PALMER

Berrett–Koehler Publishers, Inc.
a BK Life book

Berrett-Koehler Publishers, Inc.
1333 Broadway, Suite 1000
Oakland, CA 94612–1921
Tel: (510) 817–2277
Fax: (510) 817–2278
www.bkconnection.com

ORDERING INFORMATION

Quantity sales. Special discounts are available on quantity purchases by corporations, associations, and others. For details, contact the "Special Sales Department" at the Berrett-Koehler address above.

Individual sales. Berrett-Koehler publications are available through most bookstores. They can also be ordered directly from Berrett-Koehler: Tel: (800) 929-2929; Fax: (802) 864-7626; www.bkconnection.com.

Orders for college textbook / course adoption use. Please contact Berrett-Koehler: Tel: (800) 929-2929; Fax: (802) 864-7626.

Distributed to the U.S. trade and internationally by Penguin Random House Publisher Services.

Berrett-Koehler and the BK logo are registered trademarks of Berrett-Koehler Publishers, Inc.

Printed in the United States of America

Berrett-Koehler books are printed on long-lasting acid-free paper. When it is available, we choose paper that has been manufactured by environmentally responsible processes. These may include using trees grown in sustainable forests, incorporating recycled paper, minimizing chlorine in bleaching, or recycling the energy produced at the paper mill.

Library of Congress Cataloging-in-Publication Data
Names: Palmer, Parker J., author.
Title: On the brink of everything : grace, gravity, and getting old /
Parker J. Palmer.
Description: First edition. | Oakland : Berrett-Koehler Publishers, [2018]
Identifiers: LCCN 2018003613 | ISBN 9781523095438 (hardback)
Subjects: LCSH: Palmer, Parker J. | Conduct of life. | Aging. | Life. |
  BISAC: SELF-HELP / Aging. | SELF-HELP / Personal Growth / Happiness. |
  SELF-HELP / Motivational & Inspirational.
Classification: LCC BJ1589 .P35 2018 | DDC 155.67/19--dc23
LC record available at https://lccn.loc.gov/2018003613

FIRST EDITION
25 24 23 22 21 20 19 18   10 9 8 7 6 5 4 3 2 1

Project manager: Susan Geraghty
Text and cover designer: Paula Goldstein
Compositor: Andrea Reider
Copyeditor: Michele Jones
Proofreader: Sophia Ho

To Sheryl Fullerton, my editor and friend, without whom several of my books would not have been written, and publishing would not have been so life-giving for me.

—and—

To my readers—young, old, and in-between—who've been a community of meaning for me through ten books and forty years of writing.

Three essays in this book are accompanied by songs written and performed by the gifted singer-songwriter Carrie Newcomer in response to themes in those essays. All three songs can be downloaded free of charge at NewcomerPalmer.com/home.

Contents

With Gratitude

WE GROW OLD AND DIE IN THE SAME WAY WE'VE LIVED OUR LIVES. That's why this book is *not* about growing old gracefully. My life has been graced, but it certainly hasn't been graceful—I've done more than my share of falling down, getting up, and falling down again. The falling down is due to missteps and gravity. The getting up is due to grace, mediated by people to whom I owe great debts of gratitude.

My dear friend and longtime editor, Sheryl Fullerton, has been my partner in publishing since 1997. I'm forever grateful to Sheryl for her belief in me, her discerning editorial eye and her patient way of helping me get through long spells of aridity. Without her, this book would not exist.

Sharon Palmer, my wife, gets the first look at everything I write, and reads it with an artist's eyes. When I asked her how she edits my stuff, she said, "I ask three questions: Is it worth saying? Is it said clearly? Is it said beautifully?" I asked her only one question: "How do I manage to get *anything* past you?" I'm beyond grateful for Sharon—for her editorial skills and intuitive understanding of what I'm trying to do as a writer, for sharing her love of nature in a way that has enriched my life and my writing, and for the fact that we get to grow old together.

Carrie Newcomer, gifted singer-songwriter, poet, and essayist, is a dear friend and conversation partner whose sensibilities I value deeply. Drawing on our decade of dialogue about the themes explored in this book, Carrie has made a generous gift to me and to my readers: three songs based on three of those themes, available free at NewcomerPalmer.com/home. Carrie's music takes this book beyond the printed page into realms where only good music can go.

Courtney Martin's influence is laced through these pages. I met Courtney ten years ago when she was in her twenties, and we soon became friends and colleagues. Commenting on her 2010 book, *Do It Anyway,* I called her "one of our most insightful culture critics and one of our finest young writers," words that have proved prophetic. I owe Courtney deep thanks for many things, including this book's title and some of the inspiration that led me to write it.

Marcy Jackson and Rick Jackson have been treasured friends and the finest of colleagues for thirty years. In the 1990s, we laid the foundations for the Center for Courage & Renewal (CCR), whose work is now worldwide. There are no words adequate to say how blessed I am by our shared journey and by the work we've done together in service of things worth caring about.

Marcy and I have cofacilitated countless CCR retreats over the past two decades, and we cocreated a program for young leaders and activists that has enriched our lives and served a lot of young people well. Along the way, we've had a running conversation about many of the topics in this book. I'm ever grateful for her deep listening, her honest and open questions, and the care and creativity with which she approaches everyone and everything.

Rick Jackson is one of the most compassionate, generous, and socially conscious people I know. He's also one of the CCR pen pals who read my manuscript with care, and commented on it in ways that helped me sharpen it. That list includes Caryl Casbon, Cat Greenstreet, Diane Rawlins, and Judy Skeen, all of whom I'm proud to call friends and colleagues. I value their keen observations and questions as well as their encouraging affirmations.

Christine Craven, my stepdaughter, has the sharpest proofreading eye of anyone I've ever worked with. I'm grateful to her for caring about this book and going through the manuscript with a fine-tooth comb.

Many of the reflections I rewrote in order to weave this book together first appeared on the website of On Being Studios, producers of the public radio program *On Being*. Deep thanks to Trent Gillis and my dear friend Krista Tippett for inviting me to become a weekly columnist, putting me in the company of writers and readers who encourage the very best of online conversation. Special thanks to Mariah Helgeson, senior editor at On Being, whose extraordinary editorial skills have helped me become a better writer.

This is my first book with Berrett-Koehler Publishers. It's been a grand ride because of the people I've worked with, all of whom have my heartfelt thanks: Maria Jesus

Aguilo, Michael Crowley, Matt Fagaly, Kristin Frantz, Susan Geraghty, Sheri Gilbert, Paula Goldstein, Michele Jones, Neal Maillet, David Marshall, Liz McKellar, Courtney Schonfeld, Jeevan Sivasubramaniam, Mayowa Tomori, Johanna Vondeling, and Lasell Whipple. I also thank the many other B-K staff who worked quietly backstage to make the book possible. It takes a village!

Finally, I want to thank three friends whose personal knowledge of aging exceeds mine, people I want to be like if and when I grow up.

Joyce and Dick McFarland are forces of nature, deeply engaged with important social issues, full of curiosity and questions, passionate about the young, generous in every way, and brimming over with laughter and light. They embody the most important qualities I write about in this book.

Lois Boyer stood on the brink of everything with as much grace as I've ever seen. Attending her 100th birthday party in October 2017 was a joy for me. I'm sad to say that Lois died before this book was published, but she was delighted to know that this story would appear in it. At her party, Lois asked me what I'd been up to lately, and I told her about this book. "Parker," she said, "you're not old enough to write a book about aging!"

So I send this book out with humility, well aware that I'm not qualified to write it! What I am is one lucky man when it comes to family, friends, and colleagues. Over the past eight decades, I could not have found better companions for the journey.

Prelude

EVERY DAY, I GET CLOSER TO THE BRINK OF EVERYTHING. We're all headed that way, of course, even when we're young, though most of us are too busy with Important Matters to ponder our mortality. But when a serious illness or accident strikes, or someone dear to us dies—or we go to a class reunion and wonder who all those old people are—it becomes harder to ignore the drop-off that lies just over the edge of our lives.

I'll be nearly eighty when this book is published, so it shouldn't surprise me that I can sometimes see the brink from here. But it does. I'm even more surprised by the fact that I *like* being old.

Age brings diminishments, but more than a few come with benefits. I've lost the capacity for multitasking, but I've rediscovered the joy of doing one thing at a time. My thinking has slowed a bit, but experience has made it deeper and richer. I'm done with big and complex projects, but more aware of the loveliness of simple things: a talk with a friend, a walk in the woods, sunsets and sunrises, a night of good sleep.

I have tears, of course, always have and always will. But as time lengthens like a shadow behind me, and the time ahead dwindles, my overriding feeling is gratitude for the gift of life.

Above all, I like being old because the view from the brink is striking, a full panorama of my life—and a bracing breeze awakens me to new ways of understanding my own past, present, and future. As one of Kurt Vonnegut's characters says in *Player Piano*, "out on the edge you can see all kinds of things you can't see from the center."[1]

Looking back, I see why I needed the tedium *and* the inspiration, the anger *and* the love, the anguish *and* the joy. I see how it all belongs, even those days of despair when the darkness overwhelmed me. Calamities I once lamented now appear as strong threads of a larger weave, without which the fabric of my life would be less resilient. Moments of fulfillment I failed to relish in my impatience to get on to the next thing now appear as times to be recalled and savored. And I've doubled down on my gratitude for those who've helped me along with love, affirmation, hard questions, daunting challenges, compassion, and forgiveness.

Looking around at our shared world, its suffering and its promise, I see the courage with which so many live in service of the human possibility. Old age is no time to hunker down, unless disability demands it. Old is just another word for nothing left to lose, a time of life to take bigger risks on behalf of the common good.

Looking ahead to the day when I go over the brink to what Leonard Cohen calls our "invincible defeat," all I know for sure is that it's a long way down.[2] Will I spread my wings and fly, fall wordless as a rock, or flame out like a screaming banshee? I have no idea.

But of this I am certain: that I've come this far makes me one of the lucky ones. Many people never had a chance to see the view from where I stand, and I might well have been among them. I've known days when the voice of depression told me that death was a better idea than trying to carry on. For a long time, I bored my doctors, but over the past fifteen years, I've become a "person of interest" to several kinds of specialists.

So I'm not given to waxing romantic about aging and dying. I simply know that the first is a privilege and the second is not up for negotiation.

❧ ❧ ❧

In 2004, shortly after my sixty-fifth birthday, I spent an evening with friends who gave me a hard time about my generation's motto, "Never trust anyone over thirty." Amid jibes like "You've exceeded your shelf life by more than twice," someone asked, "Seriously, how do you feel about getting old?"

"I'll let you know when I get there," I said. "But I can tell you this. The Dylan Thomas poem I loved when I was young—'Do not go gentle into that good night'—no longer speaks to me."[3]

It was a late summer evening, and we had a lovely view to the west. "Look at that sunset," I went on. "It's beautiful, and it keeps getting more beautiful before things go dark. If that sun began to rise right now, we'd be shriek-ing, *Apocalypse!*, knowing that our solar system had gone bonkers, that the laws of nature had failed.

"I don't want to fight the gravity of aging. It's nature's way. I want to collaborate with it as best I can, in hopes of going down with something like the grace of that setting sun. For all the wrinkles and worry lines, it's a lovely thing simply to be one of those who's lived long enough to say, 'I'm getting old.'"

Today, I smile at the notion of "collaborating with aging." It reminds me of the exchange between the nineteenth-century transcendentalist Margaret Fuller and the writer Thomas Carlyle. "I accept the universe," proclaimed Fuller. "Gad! She'd better," replied Carlyle.[4] I'm with her in this little spat, though I do admire his wit.

We have no choice about death. But we do have choic-es to make about how we hold the inevitable—choices made difficult by a culture that celebrates youth, disparages old age, and discourages us from facing into our mortal-ity. The laws of nature that dictate the sunset dictate our demise. But how we travel the arc between our own sunrise and sundown is ours to choose: Will it be denial, defiance, or collaboration?

For many years, writing has been one of my ways of col-laborating with life. For me, writing is not about filling my head with ideas, then downloading them to the page. That's not writing; it's typing.[5] Writing is an unfolding of what's going on inside me as I talk to myself on a pad of paper or a computer, a version of talk therapy that requires neither an appointment nor a fee. This book, my tenth, is one fruit of my collaboration with aging—an offering from a fellow traveler to those who share this road, pondering as they go.

~ ~ ~

A few words about "grace, gravity, and getting old." I'm writing this Prelude in Santa Fe, New Mexico. For over a decade, my wife and I have come here in the late spring for a couple of weeks of hiking, writing, napping, eating Southwestern food, and enjoying spectacular sunsets.

At my age, the napping, eating, and sky-gazing are no stretch. But out on a mountain trail, I feel both grace and gravity more keenly than when I first came here in my mid-sixties.

The grace is that I have the health and resources to get myself out to the high desert; that, after a couple of days, my heart and lungs are still able to adjust to the 7,000-foot difference between Santa Fe and my Midwestern home; that I can stand at a trailhead and still feel confident about getting partway up, maybe even to the top of a trail that climbs from 9,000 to 10,000 feet; that every foot of the way I'm surrounded by beauty that a lot of people never get a chance to see.

But as I climb, gravity kicks in. I hike more slowly than I used to, stopping to catch my breath more often. I have to be more attentive to where I'm putting my feet lest a momentary imbalance pitch me into a fall. The tug of gravity is an inescapable part of aging. As they say, "Everything goes south." Energy, reaction time, muscle tone, the body itself—they're all headed back into the earth, as far south as it goes.

There's no antidote for the gravity that takes us to the grave. But there is a countervailing force called "levity." According to an online etymological dictionary, "In [the] old science (16th–17th Century), [levity is] the name of a force or property of physical bodies, the opposite of gravity, causing them to tend to rise."[6] For us, of course, levity means the kind of humor that eases the burden of life's gravitas, the kind G. K. Chesterton had in mind when he said, "Angels can fly because they can take themselves lightly."[7]

As Leonard Cohen writes in one of his many memorable verses, "Well, my friends are gone and my hair is grey / I ache in the places where I used to play."[8] It's all true, and the first few words are heavy. But the laugh that comes with the second line lightens the load.

Poetry also lightens the load by lifting weighty things using the leverage of metaphor. Here's an example from the poet Jeanne Lohmann, who wrote with insight and elegance until her death at age ninety-three. Her poem helps me deal with the sense of heaviness about aging that occasionally comes over me. It also helped inspire me to write this book—a meditation on aging in which I've tried to be true to gravity, to grace, and to the voice of my own experience in a way that invites the reader to listen to his or hers:

Invocation

Let us try what it is to be true to gravity,
to grace, to the given, faithful to our own voices,
to lines making the map of our furrowed tongue.
Turned toward the root of a single word, refusing

solemnity and slogans, let us honor what hides
and does not come easy to speech. The pebbles
we hold in our mouths help us to practice song,
and we sing to the sea. May the things of this world
be preserved to us, their beautiful secret
vocabularies. We are dreaming it over and new,
the language of our tribe, music we hear
we can only acknowledge. May the naming powers
be granted. Our words are feathers that fly
on our breath. Let them go in a holy direction.[9]

I hope that the words on these pages refuse "solemnity
and slogans" and "honor what hides and does not come
easy to speech." My words are no more than "feathers that
fly," but that does not matter. What matters is that they fly
"in a holy direction," the direction of life.

≈ ≈ ≈

My first book came out in 1979 when I was forty, my
ninth book in 2011 when I was seventy-two. So on average
it's taken me three or four years to write a book. Every book
has felt like a marathon, and after I finished number nine,
I felt certain I didn't have another long-distance race in me.

Toward the end of 2015, I was talking with Sheryl
Fullerton, my longtime editor and friend, who wondered
if I was working on a new book. "No," I said, "I don't
have the energy for it. But I'm really enjoying short-form
writing—brief essays and a little poetry."

Sheryl asked, "Have you thought about gathering
those essays, along with some of your poetry, editing them,

writing some new material, and weaving all of it into a book, the way you did with *Let Your Life Speak*?" The conversation that followed is a good example of how we get by with a little (or a lot) of help from our friends, just as the Beatles claimed:

Me: No, I haven't. I mean, a book has to be about *something*. My short pieces have been all over the map.

Sheryl: Um, that's not true. I know, because you've sent me a lot of those pieces over the last few years.

Me: And you think there's a theme running through them?

Sheryl *(after a brief silence)*: Parker, do you ever *read* what you write?

Me: Of course not. Why should I? I *write* the stuff. But, OK, I'll bite. What, pray tell, have I been writing about?

Sheryl: Getting old! That's what you've been writing about. Didn't you know that?

Me *(lights blinking on in my brain)*: Well, no . . . But now that you mention it, a book on aging might be interesting . . . Wow, am I ever glad I had *that* idea!

Thus was conceived this book, in which I've tried to craft a many-faceted reflection on aging from twenty-four brief essays and a number of poems, including some of my own.[10] The book is not a "guide to" or "handbook for" getting old. Instead, it's me turning the prism on my experience of aging as a way of encouraging readers to do the same with theirs. We need to reframe aging as a passage of discovery and engagement, not decline and inaction.

Since we're all aging all the time—if we're lucky—I hope the book will resonate not only with my age-mates but with people not yet certifiably old. After all, there are young people whom we rightly call "old souls." I think, for example, of my twenty-seven-year-old granddaughter, Heather Palmer, who is also one of my best friends. The journey we've shared since the day she was born has opened my eyes, mind, and heart to so much.

I turn the prism seven times in the course of these pages, refracting my experience of aging in a different light with each turn:

I. **The View from the Brink: What I Can See from Here** probes some things I'm learning as I age, especially the importance of keeping my eyes open to the experience and asking the right questions about it.

II. **Young and Old: The Dance of the Generations** focuses on creative engagement with the young. When young and old are connected like the poles of a battery, the power that's released enlivens both parties and helps light up the world.

III. **Getting Real: From Illusion to Reality** reflects on the spiritual life, which I understand as an endless effort to penetrate illusion and touch reality—a vital task at any age and an imperative for aging well.

IV. **Work and Vocation: Writing a Life** is about the voice that calls to many of us, saying, "Whatever your paid work may be, *this* is what gives you life"—the voice that has long said to me, "Write!" As we age, it's important to get clear about the difference between the jobs by which we make a living and the callings, or vocations, by which make meaning. Many elders leave or lose their jobs. But it's possible to follow a calling to the end of life, and continue to make meaning at a time when it's much needed.

V. **Keep Reaching Out: Staying Engaged with the World** makes a case for the importance of elders never ceasing to care about our shared world, and acting on what we care about—if only in our minds and hearts and via words spoken to people close at hand.

VI. **Keep Reaching In: Staying Engaged with Your Soul** is about the centrality of inner work done in silence and solitude. Knowing yourself and sinking your roots into the ground of your being are critical in old age. Becoming comfortable with silence and solitude can ease the final transition from life to death—a journey we must make alone back into the silence from which we came.

VII. **Over the Edge: Where We Go When We Die** answers the age-old question, "What happens to us after death?" My original marketing plan was simple: "Want the answer? Buy the book." But my publisher nixed that idea—something about truth in advertising. I'll simply say that, after reading Chapter VII, you'll know where heaven is, though I may be a little off with the longitude and latitude.

Welcome to the brink of everything. It takes a lifetime to get here, but the stunning view and the bracing breeze in your face make it worth the trip.

I. The View from the Brink

What I Can See from Here

Introduction

Check the *Cambridge Dictionary* online, and you'll find the phrase *on the brink* defined as "the edge of a cliff or other high area, or the point at which something good or bad will happen," followed by this example: "The company was on the brink of collapse."[1]

I'm not sure why most uses of the phrase are negative—as in on the brink of giving up, or losing my mind, or going to war—even though it can be used positively. Perhaps it's because, deep in the reptilian brain, we're afraid of falling from heights or crossing boundaries into the unknown. But isn't it possible that we're on the brink of flying free, or discovering something of beauty, or finding peace and joy?

As I said in the Prelude, I like being "on the brink of everything" because it gives me new perspectives on my past, present, and future, and new insights into the inner dynamics that shape and drive my life. The essays in this chapter explore a few inner-life findings that have taken me by surprise in recent years. Some of them have been humbling; all of them have been life-giving.

The first essay, "On the Brink of Everything," explains how I stole the title of this book from a superb piece by my friend, the writer Courtney Martin, who wrote about the wonder of watching her daughter, Maya, discover the world. Reading that essay early one winter morning, I realized something that started me down the path to writing this book: what Maya was discovering at sixteen months, I was rediscovering in my late seventies.

In the second essay, "Does My Life Have Meaning?," I recount how I learned what's wrong with that ancient and oft-asked question: when you ask the wrong question, you end up with the wrong answer. So I set out to find the right question—or at least one of them—and found one that works for me. If my question doesn't work for you, maybe my musings will encourage you to find one that does.

"Withering into the Truth" puts a positive spin on the wrinkles that come with getting old. Age gives us a chance to outgrow what William Butler Yeats called "the lying days of [our] youth" and wither into what Oliver Wendell Holmes called "the simplicity that lies on the other side of complexity."[2] I've long thought of old age as a time when all that's left is to tell the truth—trying to remember to tell it in love. It's liberating to be at a point where I no longer need to posture or pretend because I no longer feel a need to prove anything to anyone.

This chapter ends with my poem "Grand Canyon," a reflection on the many-layered lives we lead, and how every layer contributes to the majesty of the whole. I wrote the poem during a rafting trip down the Colorado River where, for nine days in a row, I experienced what the boatmen often call "another day in the ditch."

Occasionally, I find myself using that phrase at the end of a difficult day, when life has been as rough as a class 10 rapid—while all around me is the grandeur of this astonishing thing called life.

On the Brink of Everything

In March 2015, I read an essay by my friend and colleague Courtney Martin called "Reuniting with Awe."[3] It painted an exquisite picture of how her sixteen-month-old daughter, Maya, helps her see life's wonders through a toddler's eyes.

I was mesmerized by Courtney's opening line: "My daughter is on the brink of everything." That's exactly where I am today at age seventy-nine. I'm frequently awestruck as I stand on the brink of the rest of my life, including the part called death, which I sometimes think I can almost see from here.

I'd be lying if I claimed to be awed by *all* that comes with old age. Courtney wrote about Maya scooping "haphazard little bits of cottage cheese into her mouth,"

My friend Carrie Newcomer, singer-songwriter, was a conversation partner in the development of this book. As I drew close to finishing it, Carrie wrote a song titled "The Brink of Everything" as a musical blessing on these pages. For a free download, visit NewcomerPalmer.com/home.

then applauding herself between bites. My mealtime misdemeanors do not merit applause. At dinner last night, my wife grinned, pointed to her chin and said, "You've got food on your face again." Reaching for a napkin, I grumped, "I was saving it for a snack."

Courtney reported that when she takes Maya out for a walk, Maya bounces "with the delight of freedom" and "quickly swivels around" to make sure her mom is following. If I bounced and swiveled, I'd need to see my doc about repairing some mission-critical body part.

Speaking of my doc, like many people my age, I live with a couple of ongoing challenges to my health. They pose no immediate threat to my life, but it gives you pause when you start meeting more frequently with specialists, especially as you watch family members and friends and colleagues fall ill and die. And yet it's *because* of the diminishments of age, not in spite of them, that I often find myself in awe as I stand on the brink of everything.

The morning Courtney's essay was published online, I began my day by waking up, an event worthy of celebration in itself. I paused on the edge of the bed to check my balance and gather my wits, then followed a well-worn path to a small room I visit a couple of times a night.

It was a hard-frozen winter day in my part of the world, and the east-facing window was filigreed with ice. Beyond the bare trees, the horizon glowed with a crimson sunrise that, viewed through the tracery of ice, turned the window pane into stained glass. I stood there for a couple of minutes taking in that scene as if I were contemplating one of the great rose windows of Chartres Cathedral.

I went downstairs, turned up the thermostat, and began heating water for coffee. Twice-warmed by the whispering furnace and the hissing burner on the gas stove, I was thrice-warmed as I reread a handwritten letter that had arrived the day before, thanking me for a book I published when I was in my early sixties. "What you wrote about your experience of depression," said my correspondent, "helped save my life."

As I laid the letter down, I thought back on all the early mornings when, in my haste to get back to my writing, I'd failed to pause for even a few minutes to take in the loveliness of an awakening world. I've long been an obsessive writer, and before age slowed me down, my impatience about hitting the keyboard kept me from seeing the beauty around me.

Part of me regrets that. And yet, back in the day—focused laser-like on surveying and mapping what's "in here" while ignoring what's "out the window"—I wrote something that helped a stranger find new life.

Looking back, I'm awed by the way that embracing *everything*—from what I got right to what I got wrong—invites the grace of wholeness. When psychologist Florida Scott-Maxwell was eighty-five, she wrote, "You need only claim the events of your life to make yourself yours. When you truly possess all you have been and done . . . you are fierce with reality."[4]

Fierce with reality is how I feel when I'm able to say, "I am that to which I gave short shrift and that to which I attended. I am my descents into darkness and my rising again into the light, my betrayals and my fidelities, my failures and my successes. I am my ignorance and my insight, my doubts and my convictions, my fears and my hopes."

Wholeness does not mean perfection—it means embracing brokenness as an integral part of life. I'm grateful for this truth as age leads me to look back on the zigzagging, up-and-down path I've hacked out during my far-from-perfect life.

The teakettle whistled, and I filled the French press with boiling water. As I waited for the coffee to brew, I booted up my smartphone, got online, and read Courtney's essay, "Reuniting with Awe." By the time I finished, I'd begun to brew this piece, aware of how much had already awed me here on the brink of a new day.

Every hour, I'm closer to death than I was the hour before. All of us draw closer all the time, but rarely with the acute awareness that comes when old age or calamity reminds us of where we stand. I have no wise words about dying and death. I've watched one loved one die in anguish, another at peace. How I will travel that last mile is anyone's guess.

As for death's aftermath, I'm not privy to reports from the other side. But I'll know I've made it to heaven if I can get early-morning coffee there—and I have reason to believe that's a possibility. I'm told they can dark-roast beans in the Other Place.

What I know for sure is this: we come from mystery and we return to mystery. I know this, too: standing closer to the reality of death awakens my wonder at the many gifts of life.

On the morning I read Courtney's essay, those gifts were numerous. I saw the world at sunrise through my own rose window. I read a stranger's generous letter alongside a friend's evocative essay. I had the physical and mental capacity to make it down the stairs, brew coffee, go back up to my office, and begin this piece. I found a line that eventually became the title of this book. And I had a laugh with myself about coffee roasted in hell and served in heaven. The spiritual bread of life gives me a bellyache if it isn't leavened with humor.

Courtney says that her daughter "approaches the world with only one giant, indiscriminate expectation: delight me." Like sixteen-month-old Maya, I want to approach the world with only one expectation as I close in on eighty. Because I'm old enough to know that the world can delight me, *my* expectation is not of the world but of myself: delight in the gift of life and be grateful.

Does My Life Have Meaning?

> . . . all that I have written seems like straw to me.

Those are the words of Thomas Aquinas—*Saint* Thomas Aquinas to Catholics—one of the Western world's most influential theologians and philosophers. He spoke them three months before he died in 1274.[5]

Aquinas was wrestling with a question that dogs people of all sorts, from parents to plumbers to professors, people like you and me who will never achieve anything like Aquinas's fame or historical impact. It's a question asked by adults of all ages, but perhaps most urgently by elders who wonder if all those years add up to anything worthwhile: Does my life have meaning?

As I go deeper into elderhood, that question rises in me more often than it did when I was young. Sometimes, I'm able to affirm that I've made meaningful contributions in at least parts of my private and public lives. At other times, everything I've done seems as flimsy and flammable as straw.

If you've ever been downcast about the meaning of your life, you know that reassurance from others, no matter how generous, doesn't do the trick. The question of meaning is one all of us must answer for ourselves—or so I thought until 5:15 a.m. on Thursday, May 12, 2016.

I was starting my day as I often do, with coffee and poetry, when I ran across a poem on the nature of love. As I read and reread it, I began to see that brooding on the question "Does my life have meaning?" is a road to nowhere. Whether I give myself a thumbs-up or a thumbs-down, there's a flaw at the heart of the question, a flaw created by my old nemesis, the overweening ego.

Here's the poem that opened my eyes, by the Nobel Prize–winning Polish poet Czesław Milosz:

Love

Love means to learn to look at yourself
The way one looks at distant things
For you are only one thing among many.
And whoever sees that way heals his heart,
Without knowing it, from various ills.
A bird and a tree say to him: Friend.

Then he wants to use himself and things
So that they stand in the glow of ripeness.
It doesn't matter whether he knows what he serves:
Who serves best doesn't always understand.[6]

There's truth and liberation in those last two lines. No matter how clear my goals may be, the truth is that I often don't know whom or what I will end up serving.

I remember a talk I gave a long time ago. My intent was to blow the audience away, but they were not impressed, as indicated by a brief and tepid round of obligatory applause. I was young, and it took weeks to get the bitter taste of failure out of my mouth. Years later, by rare chance, I met a person who'd been in that audience. "I'm glad to meet you," he said. "I've wanted to tell you how your talk changed the way I approach teaching, and how good that change has been for me and my students."

His words were a powerful reminder that I don't and can't know the meaning of my life, let alone dictate or control it. As Milosz says, "It doesn't matter whether he [she] knows what he [she] serves." All I can control are my own intentions, and my willingness to give myself to them: may they always be to serve rather than show off.

The poet goes on to say, "Who serves best doesn't always understand." Those words are liberating because there's so much about life that's triple-wrapped in mystery. When I'm sure I know exactly what I'm doing and why—so sure that I miss vital clues about what's actually needed and what I have to offer—it's a sign that my ego's in charge, and that's dangerous. My best offerings come from a deeper, more intuitive place that I can only call my soul. Embracing the fact that there's no way to know with precision whom or what I'm serving helps free my words and actions from the ego's dominion.

Speaking of the ego, the first few lines of Milosz's poem are a direct challenge to its lust for center stage: "Love means to learn to look at yourself / The way one looks at distant things / For you are only one thing among many." Ah, yes, now I remember: I'm not the sun at the center of anyone's solar system. If I keep trying to put myself there, insisting that I am special and my life must have some sort of special meaning, I'll die in despair or in delusion.

Peace comes when I understand that I am "only one thing among many," no more and no less important than the bird and the tree Milosz writes about. There's much I don't know about birds and trees, but this I know for sure: they don't wonder or worry about whether their lives have meaning. They simply *be what they be.* In the process, they befriend people like me who are elevated simply by taking time to appreciate the gifts so freely given by the natural world.

Milosz says, "whoever sees that way heals his heart, / Without knowing it, from various ills." Time and again, that's been my experience. There's nothing like a walk in the woods, into the mountains, alongside the ocean, or out in the desert to put my life in perspective and help me take heart again. In places like that, the things of nature befriend me—just as Milosz says they will—as I settle into the comforting knowledge that I am "only one thing among many."

Then there are Milosz's beautiful words about allowing one's self and the things of the world to "stand in the glow of ripeness." Please don't ask me exactly what that means, because I don't know. But I do know this: once I understand that I'm not the sun, I can get out of the sun's way and stop casting shadows. I can step aside to let the true sun shine on everyone and everything, making all things ripe with the glow of life. This, it seems, is Milosz's ultimate definition of love, and it works for me.

At the moment, I rest easy with the notion that I don't need to ask or answer the question "Does my life have meaning?" All I need do is to keep living as one among many as well as I can, hoping to help myself and others grow ripe with life and love as we stand under the sun.

If the Big Question returns to me over the next few days or weeks, and I find myself struggling to come up with a "Yes" or dodge a "No," I won't be surprised. When it comes to jailbreaks like the one Milosz's poem gave me, I'm a lifelong recidivist.

It's not easy to subdue the overweening ego in order to free the adventuresome soul. But whenever we manage to do so, it saves us grief and serves the world well. So if you see me on the street one day, quietly muttering "only one thing among many, only one thing among many," you'll know I'm still working on it. Or it's still working on me.

Withering into the Truth

The Coming of Wisdom with Time

Though leaves are many, the root is one;
Through all the lying days of my youth
I swayed my leaves and flowers in the sun,
Now may I wither into the truth.

—WILLIAM BUTLER YEATS[7]

Every year, when friends say they don't know what to give me for my birthday, I respond with the same old bad joke they've heard from me before. They sigh, roll their eyes, and change the subject. (This is a perk that comes with age: repeat yourself so often that folks think you're getting dotty, when in fact you're fending off unwanted conversations.)

Q: What do you give a person who has everything?
A: Penicillin.

I don't need gifts of a material nature. But I do need to remember a few things I've learned during nearly eight decades of life. So here's a collection of six lessons as birthday gifts to myself. If one or two of them turn out to be gifts for you, that will make my next birthday even happier.

1. The Yeats poem at the head of this essay names something I don't want to forget. Actively embracing aging gives me a chance to move beyond "the lying days of my youth" and to "wither into the truth"—if I resist the temptation to Botox my withering.

My youthful "lies" weren't intentional. I just didn't know enough about myself, the world, and the right relationship of the two to tell the truth. So what I said on those subjects often came from my ego, a notorious liar. Coming to terms with the soul-truth of who I am—with my complex and confusing mix of darkness and light—has required my ego to shrivel up. Nothing shrivels a person better than age. That's what all those wrinkles are about.

Whatever truthfulness I've achieved on this score comes not from some spiritual practice that helps me summon the courage to face myself honestly. It comes from having my ego so broken down and composted by life that I found myself compelled to cry uncle and say, "OK, I get it. I'm way less than perfect."

2. Poetry has redemptive power for me, as it does for millions of people. Poets like Rainer Maria Rilke, Mary Oliver, Wendell Berry, Naomi Shihab Nye, William Stafford, and Gerard Manley Hopkins have provided life jackets to keep me from drowning, ballast to keep me from ascending to altitudes where there's not enough oxygen to support life, and maps to keep me from getting lost in the wilderness. By following Emily Dickinson's advice to "tell the truth but tell it slant," good poets have a way of sneaking up on me to deliver messages I might have tried to dodge if I'd seen them coming.[8]

I write poetry as well as read it because it's one of the best forms of self-therapy I know. Here's a poem that came to me years ago while I was trudging down a country road past a plowed field, deeply depressed and wondering if *this* was the day. It's a poem that, over time, helped me find my way back to life.

Harrowing

The plow has savaged this sweet field
Misshapen clods of earth kicked up
Rocks and twisted roots exposed to view
Last year's growth demolished by the blade.

I have plowed my life this way
Turned over a whole history
Looking for the roots of what went wrong
Until my face is ravaged, furrowed, scarred.

Enough. The job is done.
Whatever's been uprooted, let it be
Seedbed for the growing that's to come.
I plowed to unearth last year's reasons—

The farmer plows to plant a greening season.

"Harrowing" doesn't merit a place in the Western literary canon. But because it helped me emerge from a deadly darkness into a "greening season," it's canonical to me.

3. Through ten books and hundreds of essays, I've written hundreds of thousands of sentences, some of them long enough to wrap around a giant redwood. But perhaps the most important sentence I've ever written is that one word, "Enough."

Said on the right occasion, that word can safeguard the soul, and saying it comes more easily with age. These days I say "enough" without hesitation to anything that's not life-giving—whether it's frenzy and overwork, a personal prejudice, an unhealthy relationship, a societal cruelty or injustice, the feckless exercise of power in fields from religion to politics, or the racism, sexism, xenophobia, and crypto-fascism sickening the US body politic.

When I was young, saying "enough" often seemed risky. I've known people who lost favor, friends, reputations, money, and livelihoods for saying, "This far and no more." But risk looks different from the vantage of old age. More than fearing the cost of taking risks for the things I care about, I fear aging into subservience to the worst impulses in and around me.

I'm among the very fortunate ones whose material needs are largely met, so I don't have to worry about losing things that some folks require for survival. For people like me, the notion that old age is a time to dial it down and play it safe is a cop-out. Those of us who are able should be raising hell on behalf of whatever we care about: freedom's just another word for not needing to count the cost.

4. One thing I care about is the younger generation and the world they're coming into, a world they're helping remake. To care about them, I find, is also to care for my own well-being.

Psychologist Erik Erikson said that en route to old age, we face a critical choice between "generativity" and "stagnation."[9] Generativity means something more than creativity. It means turning toward the rising generation, offering whatever we know that they might find useful—and, even more important, learning from them. I talk and work with young people as often as I can, and always come away the better for it.

Several years ago, I held a two-day meeting in our home with a small group of young adults less than half my age. I listened as they talked about how the emerging world looks from where they stand. At some point, I said something like this:

> I feel like I'm standing partway down the curvature of the earth, while you're close to the top of that curve looking at a horizon that I can't see. I need to know what you're seeing, because whatever's on that horizon is coming at me as well. Please let me know what it is—and when you do, speak loudly and clearly so I can hear what you're saying!

Hint to my age-mates: next time you think, "I'm over the hill," say to yourself, "Nah, I'm just standing farther down the curvature of the earth."

5. Most older folks I know fret about unloading material goods they've collected over the years, stuff that was once useful to them but now prevents them from moving freely about their homes. There are precincts in our basement where a small child could get lost for hours.

But the junk I really need to jettison in my old age is psychological junk—such as longtime convictions about what gives my life meaning that no longer serve me well. For example, who will I be when I can no longer do the work that has been a primary source of identity for me for the past half century?

I won't know the answer until I get there. But on my way to that day, I've found a question that's already brought me a new sense of meaning. I no longer ask, "What do I want to let go of, and what do I want to *hang on to*?" Instead I ask, "What do I want to let go of, and what do I want to *give myself to*?"

The desire to "hang on" comes from a sense of scarcity and fear. The desire to "give myself" comes from a sense of abundance and generosity. That's the kind of truth I want to wither into.

6. Sooner or later, "withering into truth" culminates in death, the ultimate form of withering and perhaps the ultimate source of truth. Who knows? Maybe death will be as the poet Lucille Clifton has it in her remarkable poem about her husband's death:

the death of fred clifton
11/10/84
age 49

i seemed to be drawn
to the center of myself
leaving the edges of me
in the hands of my wife
and I saw with the most amazing
clarity
so that I had not eyes but
sight,

and, rising and turning
through my skin,
there was all around not the
shapes of things
but oh, at last, the things
themselves.[10]

I have no idea what, if anything, I will learn from dying. This is all I know for sure: I have no bad memories of wherever I came from when I arrived on this planet, so I have no good reason to fear where I'm going when I take my leave.

Besides, I know exactly where I'm going: to the Boundary Waters Canoe Area up along the Minnesota-Ontario border (48°N, 91°W), a wild and holy place where I've spent summer's end every year for the past two decades. Whenever I'm there, I think, "*This* is heaven." All that's left is to figure out how to bring a canoe along.

I may not have heaven's latitude and longitude exactly right. But one way or another, we're all going to end up in Mother Nature's arms as our atoms recombine with the stuff from which they came. When I'm in need of the comfort that comes from that undeniable fact, all I need to do is to take another walk in the woods, or a hike into the mountains, or a stroll alongside the ocean, or a trek in the desert. Such ineffable beauty, such surpassing grace!

Grand Canyon

They say the layered earth rose up
ancient rock leviathan
trailing ages in its wake
lifting earth-mass toward the sun
and coursing water cut the rock away
to leave these many-storied walls
exposé of ages gone
around this breathless emptiness
more wondrous far
than earth had ever known

My life has risen layered too
each day each year in turn has left
its fossil life and sediments
evidence of lived and unlived hours
the tedium the anguish yes the joy
that some heart-deep vitality
keeps pressing upward
toward the day I die

And Spirit cuts like water through it all
carving out this emptiness
so inner eye can see
the soaring height of canyon walls within
walls whose very color, texture, form

redeem in beauty all my life has been
the darkness and the light, the false, the true
while deep below the living waters run
cutting deeper through my parts
to resurrect my grave-bound heart
making, always making, all things new.

—PARKER J. PALMER

II. Young and Old

The Dance of the Generations

Introduction

Since my mid-twenties, I've been lucky to work with people younger than I. When I began teaching college, I had only a few years on my students—but for some inexplicable reason, the age gap between us grew wider as time went by. For the past three decades, as a workshop and retreat facilitator, I've often worked with people twenty to forty years my junior. Without these relationships across the generations, my life would have been so much poorer, and my aging would have been deprived of a source of vitality.

When young and old connect, it's like joining the poles of a battery. Together, we generate energy for personal and social change that an age-segregated society cuts off. The social conditions that keep us apart aren't going to change any time soon. But elders can reach out to the young, many of whom yearn for us to take an interest in them, their fears, their dreams, and their futures.

The first essay in this chapter, "The Music of Mentoring," comes from my own experience of being a mentor. But its roots reach back to the years when I was mentored, to the elders who graced my life and helped me find my path when I was young. Mentors kept showing up for me until I was in my mid-thirties—then they stopped coming.

I grieved that fact for a while, until I saw the secret hidden in plain sight: it was *my* turn to pay it forward by serving as a mentor for members of the rising generation. Then I found another secret hidden behind the first one: when I help young people flourish, they return the favor.

"Welcome to the Human Race" is a letter to my friend and colleague Courtney Martin. For several years, she and I have been online weekly columnists at On Being Studios. One week, Courtney wrote an open letter to me about the struggles that people in their mid-thirties, especially women, have around questions of purpose, and invited me to respond with an open letter to her.

"Living from the Inside Out" is a commencement speech I gave to the Class of 2015 at Naropa University in Boulder, Colorado. As a rule, I don't enjoy giving graduation talks. I feel like a stranger who's crashing a party of family and friends where people are polite, but would just as soon I wasn't there. So I do the job my host has asked me to do as well as I can, knowing that my *real* job is to get out of the way so the party can begin. But the Naropa University commencement felt genuinely welcoming, and it gave me another chance to help generate some intergenerational electricity.

"November 22nd" is a poem I wrote on the forty-fifth anniversary of the assassination of John F. Kennedy. On that date in 1963, I was a twenty-four-year-old graduate student at the University of California, Berkeley. I remember exactly where I was when I got the news, of course: Cody's Bookstore on Telegraph Avenue. In that moment, I began my journey from youthful naiveté to a more tragic view of life, while setting off on a quest to find meaning beyond the madness.

The Music of Mentoring

Every spring, commencement speakers take the stage across the country to tell the graduates, "Our hopes for the future are in your hands." I have an urgent message for these speakers: in the name of God, don't do it!

It's unfair to lay all responsibility for the future on the younger generation. After all, the problems they face are partly due to the fact that we, their elders, screwed up. Worse still, it's not true that the young alone are in charge of what comes next. *We*—young and old together—hold the future in *our* hands. If our common life is to become more compassionate, creative, and just, it will take an intergenerational effort.

Let's stop talking about "passing the baton" to the young as we elders finish running our laps. Since most of us are more skilled at sitting than at running, let's change the metaphor and invite young adults to join the orchestra. As we sit together, we can help them learn to play their instruments—while they help us learn the music of the emerging world, which they hear more clearly than we do. Together we can compose something lovelier and more alive than the current cacophony, something in which dissonance has a place but does not dominate.

Many people, said Oliver Wendell Holmes, "die with all their music in them."[1] I was saved from that sad fate by a series of mentors who reached out to me when I was young to help me find my own music and learn how to play it. Now I have chance after chance to pass that gift along to the next generation, whose music is waiting to be heard. So does every elder who's within reach of a younger person.

When I ask people to tell me about their great mentors, they almost always respond with words akin to what I've said about my own:

> My mentors saw more in me than I saw in myself. They evoked that "more" in many ways—challenging me, cheering for me, helping me understand that failure is part of the deal. Then my mentors opened doors for me, or at least pointed me toward them. When I was willing to walk through those doors, I found purpose and meaning. My mentors changed my life.

Age and experience have taught me that mentoring is not a one-way street. It's a mutuality in which two people evoke the potentials in each other. To borrow a phrase from theologian Nelle Morton, mentoring is about "hearing one another to speech."[2] Equally important, mentoring gives us a chance to welcome one another into a relationship that honors our vulnerability and our need for each other.[3] Mentoring is a gift exchange in which we elders receive at least as much as we give, often more.

As elders, we know—or should know—that we have gifts to offer the young. In many cases, we've been where they are and done what they're doing. We've fallen down and gotten back up, learned from our failures, lived to tell the tale, and gone on to get a few things right. When the moment comes to share our stories with the young, we can help them find their way through the thickets of life and work.

I once led a daylong faculty workshop focused on the optimal conditions for student learning. At lunch, I sat with seven professors, all men. One began talking about how he hit the wall in college when he failed the organic chemistry course that stood between him and the medical degree his father wanted him to get. "It was the most devastating moment of my young life," he said, "but it led me toward a career in literature that has fed my soul."

Everyone at the table, including me, had a story about a youthful failure that morphed into fulfillment. As people got ready to return to the workshop, I asked, "How many of you have told your story of 'creative failure' to your students?"

When no one's hand went up, I said, "Your classrooms are filled with students who feel like failures in some area of their lives, maybe in your course. Your stories could help some of them catch a glimmer of hope. So please, please tell them when the moment is ripe."

We elders have gifts for the young, but the young are often unaware of the gifts they have for us. They rarely understand, for example, that when they approach an older person for mentoring, they assuage our fear that we're over the hill and out of the game, that younger folks regard us as irrelevant. Few people in their twenties know the power of saying to someone like me—who's seen twenty nearly four times—"I want to learn from you."

The young also bring gifts of energy, vision, and hope that hard experience has stolen from me, often without my knowing it. They soften my cynicism when I see them taking on a problem I regard as intractable, approaching it from a new angle that just might work. "Once more into the breach," I think, "as long as I can go with them."

I disagree with elders who say, "We must keep the young from making the same mistakes we made." They're going to make mistakes, but they're not going to make the same ones we did. They are not us, their world is not the same as the one in which we grew up, and it's possible that they're wiser than we were.

So let's share our experience with younger folks in ways that help them step up, not back. Then let's walk alongside them as they "do it anyway," which happens to be the title of a fine book by Courtney Martin.[4] In it, she tells the stories of eight young activists who do what needs doing even when the smart money says it can't be done. When they fall down, as change agents invariably do, we can help them get up, or simply be inspired as we watch them do it on their own. Maybe their next try will be one of those delicious moments when the smart money proves itself dumb.

There's much more to be said about the gifts the young offer the old, including the way many of them walk so unselfconsciously across the so-called lines of difference between us, as if deep down we had more in common than appears on the surface. Which we do, of course.

But rather than enumerating all the gifts the young have to offer, I'll close by naming one more that too often goes unseen and unsung. Unlike many folks my age, the young people I work with waste no time grieving the collapse of the "old order," of the religious, educational, vocational, and political structures that helped form their elders' lives. When today's young adults were born, many of those institutions were well on their way to becoming dysfunctional.

Instead of bemoaning what's on its way out or already gone, many of the young adults I know are inventing forms of work and life that hold great promise—from political movements, to religious life, to staying connected in communities of meaning. They're also crafting independent careers and creating alternative workplaces, declaring their freedom from corporations that force people into rigid roles and treat their employees as replaceable cogs in a machine.

That freedom allows them to be loyal to their own gifts and visions, and to the relationships required to bring those visions to life. I find it inspiring to hang out with people who aren't bemoaning the loss of what no longer serves us well. Instead, they're exploring possibilities that we, young and old together, can midwife into life.

As I was working on this essay, one of my mentees reminded me that I'd written about mentoring in my 1997 book, *The Courage to Teach,* a fact I'd forgotten. (Here's another gift the young offer the old—they serve as auxiliary memory banks.) Now that I'm old enough to mix metaphors without caring what my English teachers say, I'm going to quote from that book, and invite the young to join us elders in "an ancient dance" instead of "the orchestra:"

> Mentors and apprentices are partners in an ancient human dance, and one of teaching's great rewards is the daily chance it gives us to get back on the dance floor. It is the dance of the spiraling generations, in which the old empower the young with their experience and the young empower the old with new life, reweaving the fabric of the human community as they touch and turn.[5]

Either way, orchestra or dance, intergenerational rhythms can move our hearts, our minds, and our feet—and might even help move the world to a better place.

Welcome to the Human Race

Dear Courtney,

I have many reasons to treasure our friendship. Among other things, you've invited me into your world, an act of

---

For several years, Courtney Martin and I have had weekly columns at On Being Studios. In one of her columns, Courtney wrote me an open letter based on conversations in her women's group, titled "Dear Parker: Purpose with a Capital P" (see http://tinyurl.com/ybrxk22h), and invited me to respond. This is what I wrote.

trust, which has made my world larger, a true gift. You and your thirty-something friends have opened my eyes to realities and possibilities that someone like me—a white, straight male who's more than twice your age—might otherwise have missed. I'm ever grateful.

At the end of your letter, you ask me (with a grin) to make you wiser. That's way above my pay grade. We both know that everyone has inner wisdom, and that one of the best ways to evoke it is in dialogue. When we knock down the walls that keep us apart (e.g., gender and age), and meet in that in-between space, we all have a chance to wise up. Already, in this exchange of letters, I've grown in my understanding of the questions you raised, questions about women and men and the different paths we walk.

As I read your account of the young women in your women's group—some of whom lament that they don't have a compelling sense of purpose—two feelings rise up in me.

I feel angry, again, at a society that makes so many people believe that they are "not enough" by devaluing certain roles and discouraging certain people from pursuing their goals. At the same time, I feel hope in the fact that you and your friends talk openly and honestly about your pain and its sources. That's a vital step in caring for personal well-being *and* in animating every social change movement I know anything about.

Regarding your friends' lack of a sense of purpose, you wrote, "We don't wake up every morning and leap out of bed for work that is easy to express in a sound bite and directed and in pursuit of one clear goal."

Honestly, if someone told me she woke up that way, I'd tell her to stop marketing her life and start living it. I'm one of those "diffuse" people you wrote about—I have a lot of irons in a lot of fires. When I'm asked for the "elevator speech" that sums up my work, I respond, "I always take the stairs, so I don't have an elevator speech. If you'd like to walk with me a while, I'd love to talk." I don't know of a life worth living or work worth doing that can be reduced to a sound bite.

The only story I know well is my own, so let me return briefly to the thrilling days of yesteryear. When I was in my thirties, "purpose" was very unclear to me—my vocation didn't begin to feel coherent until I was in my early fifties. At thirty, all I knew for sure was that I didn't want my life and work to be defined and bound by big organizations. So I worked in marginal places, turning down invitations that might get me embedded in "centers of power."

For example, with a PhD in hand, I became a community organizer instead of a university professor. I made little money and feared dropping off the professional radar, but I valued my creative freedom more than money or status. (I had a family, a wife and three children, and I did not have a trust fund to fall back on. But clearly I had a safety net in terms of race, gender, and class privilege, along with a debt-free degree, financed by a fellowship.)

I never saw my vocational journey in terms of "achieving great things." I saw it then as I see it now: a series of probes into my gifts and the needs of the world, trying to discover where they might intersect. Some of those probes took me into the light, and others took me into dark places. I've come to regard my probes as "experiments with truth," to borrow Gandhi's description of his life. Like all experiments, some succeeded and some failed.[6]

You wrote, "I was looking around this table at these women, all of them doing incredible work in the world while also being loving mothers, friends, partners, neighbors, and thinking, 'It's crazy that this group of women doesn't see themselves as having purpose.'" My hunch is that a lot of your women friends—certainly the ones I've met—are making probes of the sort I made, "living the questions" in ways that have meaning right now and will someday take them into meaningful answers.[7]

I wouldn't try to talk your friends out of their feelings, of course. As you well know, feeling are feelings, not abstract ideas, and must be honored as such. But I might invite your friends to examine their feelings, to see what insights they offer into their souls, their lives, and their work. If I wanted to give them a gentle nudge, I might suggest that they congratulate themselves for refusing to foreclose prematurely on purpose, as this society keeps pressing young people to do.

Courtney, you asked some big questions about gender differences in how we hold vocation and values. As a recovering sociologist, I have little confidence in big generalizations on questions of that sort. All I know for sure is that the men I know best have struggled with questions of purpose as much as your women friends do.

Yes, this society opens more vocational paths for men than for women, and offers men bigger material rewards for walking them. That's institutional sexism, which must be eradicated, as must all the other "-isms" that go hand in hand with it. But in my view, few of the well-paved paths in this society are "paths with a heart," paths that lead to meaning. Paths of that sort have to be hacked out of complexity and confusion by men and women alike—and I regard you and some of your age-mates as trailblazers.

Among the men I know, few are so consumed by an egotistical sense of singular purpose that they ignore all else that's important in life. But that's not to say that all is well among us. Far from it. I've seen too many men lose their sense of identity—and sometimes their integrity—as their work roles diminish or disappear.

I don't believe this happens because we men think too much of ourselves. It happens because we haven't done the inner work required to develop a sense of self that's grounded in who we *are* rather than what we *do*. When men lose sight of true north, it's more from inner emptiness than from self-importance. That's when some men go "looking for love in all the wrong places"—places that sometimes involve exploitative sex and substance abuse but more often involve lust for power, wealth, and/or fame.

The most common spiritual malady among the men I know is not the kind of ego inflation that "disappears" everything else in their lives. It's what was once called "melancholy" that, when it grows deep enough, can cause one's sense of self to disappear. As you know, I speak from experience.

This could change, I think, if more men came together—as you and your friends do—to talk vulnerably about their frustrations, fears, and hopes. There's a reason why one of the best-known books on male depression is titled *I Don't Want to Talk About It.*[8]

Your comments about men's moral failings lead me to say a few words not about others but about myself. Something about "casting the first stone," as I recall. You know me pretty well, so you know that I have a lifetime supply of flaws and faults. I have a hunch that the best words I've ever written have been written from and to my own mixed condition, written in hopes they might speak to others who know that being human means being broken and yet whole.

The word *integrity* comes from a root that means "intact." At bottom, it has to do with being "integral," whole and undivided—which means embracing our brokenness as an integral part of life. Do men compromise their integrity more than women? I don't know, though I'm inclined to think we share this particular weakness as part of the human condition.

What I do know is that I yearn for the day when men and women alike can sit with people they trust, including each other, and share the journey toward broken-wholeness.

I'll close with one of the big questions I'm holding as I enter the late autumn of my life: Given all my mess-ups, how have I managed to survive *myself*? As age gives me an occasional glimpse into "the simplicity on the other side of complexity," a few answers become clear: grace and forgiveness, the unconditional love of family and friends, and the openness of folks who've shared their stories with me, helping me to feel less alone in my struggles.[9] More grace. More forgiveness. More loving and open friends.

Courtney, you are among the people who, in one way or another, have blessed me with the most healing words I know, words spoken not in spite of but because of my mess-ups: "Welcome to the human race!"

Maybe my main purpose in life is to pass on those words to people who need them as much as I do, so that they can pass them along to others—and all of us can get on with offering our gifts to the world.

Maybe that's what you and your friends are already doing for each other, and for the people whose lives you touch.

With love and gratitude,
Parker

Living from the Inside Out

I'm grateful to be with you today at a university that's been pioneering in contemplative teaching and learning for the past forty years. The seeds you've been planting are now growing across American higher education in ways no one could have predicted when Naropa was founded. It's a mode of higher education that benefits not only you personally but the larger world as well.

It's an honor to share this important moment in the lives of the Class of 2015. I've brought two modest graduation gifts with me. The first is a collection of six brief

This is an edited version of my commencement address to the Class of 2015 at Naropa University, Boulder, Colorado. The talk can be viewed on YouTube at http://tinyurl.com/y8bjdzce.

suggestions about the road ahead of you. The second is a promise to stop talking in about twelve minutes so you can get on that road sooner rather than later.

My first suggestion is simple: be reckless when it comes to affairs of the heart. Now, lest someone think I'm trying to corrupt America's youth—I'm looking at you, parents and grandparents!—what I mean is to fall madly in love with life. Be passionate about some part of the natural and/or human worlds, and take risks on its behalf, no matter how vulnerable they make you.

No one ever died saying, "I'm so glad for the self-centered, self-serving, and self-protective life I lived." Offer yourself to the world—your energies, your gifts, your visions, your spirit—with openhearted generosity.

But understand that when you live this way, you will soon learn how little you know and how easy it is to fail. To grow in love and service, you must value ignorance as much as knowledge and failure as much as success.

This is ironic advice on a day when we celebrate your success at passing a rigorous test of knowledge. But clinging to what you already know is the path to an unlived life. So cultivate beginner's mind, walk straight into your not-knowing, and take the risk of failing and falling, again and again—then getting up to learn again and again. That's the path to a life lived large in the service of love, truth, and justice.

Second, as you integrate ignorance and failure into your knowledge and success, do the same with all the alien parts of yourself. Take everything that's bright and beautiful in you and introduce it to your shadow side. Let your altruism meet your egotism, your generosity meet your greed, your joy meet your grief.

Everyone has a shadow, even high-minded people like us. *Especially* high-minded people like us! But when you are able to say, "I am all of the above, my shadow as well as my light," the shadow's power is put in service of the good. As a person who's made three deep dives into his own shadow side, and lived to serve another day, I don't speak lightly of this. I simply know it is true.

When you acknowledge and embrace all that you are, you give yourself a gift that will benefit the rest of us as well. Our world is in desperate need of leaders who live what Socrates called "an examined life." In critical areas like politics, religion, business, and mass media, too many leaders refuse to name and claim their shadow because they don't want to look weak. With shadows that go unexamined and unchecked, they use their power heedlessly in ways that harm countless people and undermine public trust in our major institutions.

If you value self-knowledge, you will become the leaders we need to help renew this society. But if, for some reason, you choose to live an unexamined life, I beg of you: do not take a job that involves other people!

Third, as you welcome whatever you find alien within yourself, extend that same welcome to whatever you find alien in the outer world. I don't know any virtue more important these days than hospitality to the stranger, to those we perceive as "other" than us.

The old majority in this society—people who look like me—is on its way out. By 2045, the majority of Americans will be people of color. Many in the old majority fear that fact—and their fear, shamelessly manipulated by too many political misleaders, is bringing us down.

The renewal this nation needs will not come from people who are afraid of "otherness" in race, ethnicity, religion, or sexual orientation. Because of that fear, our once-vital society is gridlocked and stagnant, if not actively regressing. Our main hope for renewal is diversity welcomed and embraced.

I recently met a professor who left a predominantly white college to teach undocumented youth in Southern California. When I asked him how it was going, he said, "Best move I ever made. My previous students felt entitled and demanded to be entertained. My undocumented students are hungry to learn, hard working, and courageous enough to keep moving beyond their comfort zones."

America will be renewed by people with those qualities. And if we who have privilege and power will welcome them, collaborate with them, and help remove the obstacles in their way, the years ahead will be full of promise for all of us.

Fourth, take on big jobs worth doing, jobs like the spread of love, peace, and justice. That means refusing to be seduced by our cultural obsession with being effective as measured by short-term results. We all want our work to make a difference. But if we take on the big jobs and our only measure of success is the next quarter's bottom line, we'll end up disappointed, dropping out, and in despair.

Think of someone you respect because he or she lived a life devoted to high values: a Rosa Parks, a Nelson

Mandela, or someone known only to a few. When that person died, was he or she able to say, "I'm sure glad I took on *that* job because now everyone can check it off their to-do list"? No, our heroes take on impossible jobs and stay with them for the long haul because they live by a standard that supersedes effectiveness.

The name of that standard is "faithfulness"—faithfulness to your gifts, to the needs of the world, and to offering your gifts to whatever needs are within your reach.

The tighter we cling to the norm of effectiveness, the smaller the tasks we'll take on, because they are the only ones that get short-term results. Public education is a tragic example. We no longer care about *educating children*—a big job that's never done. We care only about getting kids to pass tests with measurable results, whether or not those tests measure what matters. In the process, we're crushing the spirits of a lot of good teachers and vulnerable kids: there are millions of kids in this country who long to be treasured, not measured.

Care about being effective, of course. But care even more about being faithful, as countless teachers do—faithful to your calling and to the true needs of those entrusted to your care. You won't get the big jobs done in your lifetime. But if, at the end of the road, you can say, "I was faithful," you can check out with a sense of satisfaction.

Fifth, since suffering as well as joy comes with being human, I urge you to remember this: *violence is what happens when we don't know what else to do with our suffering.* Sometimes we aim that violence at ourselves—as in overwork that leads to burnout or various forms of substance abuse. Sometimes we aim that violence at other people: racism, sexism, and homophobia often come from people trying to relieve their suffering by claiming superiority over others.

The good news is that suffering can be transformed into something that brings life, not death. It happens every day. At my age, I know many people who've suffered the loss of the dearest person in their lives. At first, they go into deep grief, certain that their lives will never again be worth living. But then they slowly awaken to the fact that—not in spite of their loss but *because* of it—they've become bigger, more compassionate people, with more capacity of heart to take in other people's sorrows and joys.

These are brokenhearted people, but their hearts have been broken open rather than broken apart. So every day, exercise your heart by taking in life's pains and joys. That kind of exercise will make your heart supple, so that when it breaks—which it surely will—it will break not into a fragment grenade but into a greater capacity for love.

Finally, I quote Saint Benedict, who said, "Daily keep your death before your eyes." That may sound like a morbid practice, but I assure you it isn't. If you hold a healthy awareness of your own mortality, your eyes will be opened to the glory and grandeur of life. And that will evoke all of the virtues I've named, as well as those I haven't, such as hope, generosity and gratitude.

If the unexamined life is not worth living, it's equally true that the unlived life is not worth examining. So I'll close with this brief quote from the writer Diane Ackerman, who reminds us to live—truly live—our lives:

The great affair, the love affair with life, is to live as variously as possible, to groom one's curiosity like a high-spirited thoroughbred, climb aboard, and gallop over the thick, sun-struck hills every day. Where there is no risk, the emotional terrain is flat and unyielding, and, despite all its dimensions, valleys, pinnacles, and detours, life will seem to have none of its magnificent geography, only a length. It began in mystery, and it will end in mystery, but what a savage and beautiful country lies in between.[10]

Once again, a deep bow to the Class of 2015. To each and every one of you, traveling mercies and many blessings as you make the journey from one mystery to the next and the next and the next.

November 22nd

On this day long years ago, our promising
young president was killed. He was far too young
to die and I too young to watch my world unravel
as it did. I grieved my loss, our loss, then started
to reweave—a work, a life, a world—not knowing
then what I know now: the world unravels always,
and it must be rewoven time and time again.

You must keep collecting threads—threads of meaning,
threads of hope, threads of purpose, energy and will—
along with all the knowledge, skill that every weaver needs.
You must keep on weaving—stopping sometimes only
to repair your broken loom—weave a cloak of warmth
and light against the dark and cold, a cloak in which
to wrap whoever comes to you in need—the world
with all its suffering, those near at hand, yourself.

And, if you are lucky, you will find along the way
the thread with which you can reweave your own
tattered life, the thread that more than any other
laces us with warmth and light, making both the
weaver and the weaving true—the red thread
they call Love, the thread you hold, then
hand along, saying to another, "You."

—Parker J. Palmer

III. Getting Real

From Illusion to Reality

⌒

Introduction

I took a run at "becoming spiritual" in my early thirties. Raised in the mainline Protestant tradition, I had studied religion in college, theological seminary, and graduate school. Intellectually, I had no problem embracing some of Christianity's key tenets, such as grace, forgiveness, incarnation, and life overcoming death. Nor did I have any problem taking a pass on the arrogantly judgmental parts of some streams of Christian tradition, or affirming the vital role of science in our lives. I've always understood faith and reason to be partners, not enemies.

But I yearned for something deeper and truer than a head full of religious ideas, no matter how sound. I wanted a lived experience of a life that was less messy than the one I had, full as it was of confusions and contradictions that fell far short of "spiritual." Or so I thought.

One day, I listened to a taped talk that Thomas Merton, the Trappist monk, had given to a roomful of would-be monks at the Abbey of Gethsemane, where

Merton was novice master. Addressing the super-pious young seekers in his care, Merton said, "Men, before you can have a spiritual life, you've got to have a life!"

Those incisive words—the monastic equivalent of "Get a life!"—laid bare my false notion that "becoming spiritual" meant leaping from the muck of my daily life into godlike clarity and purity. Merton's words hit me like a one-two punch: "Wow, he's right, I need to get a life. No, wait! I've already got one! It's a god-awful mess, but I think he's saying that only there can I find my spiritual path."

The spiritual journey is an endless process of engaging life as it is, stripping away our illusions about ourselves, our world, and the relationship of the two, moving closer to reality as we do. That process begins with losing the illusion that spirituality will float us above the daily fray. Reality may be hard, but it's a safer place to live than in our illusions, which will always fail us, and at no point is that more true than in old age. Death is, after all, the end of all our illusions—so why not do what we can to lose our illusions before death strips them from us? That way we are less likely to die disappointed or in despair.

The first essay in this chapter, "Contemplative by Catastrophe," is a confession. As much as I envy people who practice spiritual disciplines that allow them to spot illusions before they get lost in them, I seem to need to get lost before I can be found. I generally do my contemplation after the train wreck, not before.

"A Friendship, a Love, a Rescue" is about my long-time relation to Thomas Merton, who has long been my most important spiritual friend and guide. I knew nothing about Merton until the year after he died. All of our meetings have taken place between the covers of books, or in moments when his words or something of his spirit come back to me. But I feel his presence as closely as I feel that of my face-to-face companions.

"Down Is the Way to Well-Being" takes a closer look at the notion that the spiritual life has nothing to do with getting "up, up and away" from the messiness of everyday life, and everything to do with staying rooted in "the ground of our being," no matter how muddy it may be.

"Notes from a Week in the Winter Woods" comprises excerpts from a bare-bones journal I kept while on one of my annual January retreats. There's nothing like a life-threatening subzero Wisconsin day to keep a person grounded in reminders of mortality.

"Welcome Home" is a poem I wrote about a moment on a walk in the hard-frozen woods—a moment when I broke through the fearful illusion that I'm not worthy of being here, back into the truth that I am, as we all are. That's a truth we need to know before we die.

Contemplative by Catastrophe

I was about thirty when I first felt drawn to the contemplative life. Inspired by reading Thomas Merton, the Trappist monk, I had visions of joining a monastic community. I thought the Abbey of Gethsemani, where Merton spent half his life, would be just right. Compared to Washington, DC—where I was caught up in the frenzy of my work as a community organizer—life at Gethsemani amid the wooded hills of Kentucky sounded idyllic.

Unfortunately, there were several major obstacles between monkhood and me. I was married, the father of three children; had a job on which my family depended; and was considerably more Quaker than Catholic. Clearly, my "visions" of a monastic life were hallucinations. So instead of applying to become a novice at Gethsemani, I ordered one of the abbey's famous fruitcakes, which are soaked and aged in fine Kentucky bourbon.*

Fortified with fruitcake, I went in search of some way to live as a contemplative amid the world's madness. Over the next few years, I read about the mystical stream that runs through all of the world's wisdom traditions. I attended guided retreats and experimented with several popular contemplative practices. But, with the exception of the Quaker meeting for worship, I couldn't find a practice compatible with my temperament, religious inclinations, and life situation.

---

*On Nov. 2, 2015, my friend Sharon Salzberg posted a superb essay on the *On Being* blog, "The Irony of Attachment" (http://tinyurl.com /y9fzl8nh). She told of the Dalai Lama receiving a gift of Trappist cheese while visiting the Abbey of Gethsemani, later telling the monks that he wished they'd given him a fruitcake instead. Sharon wrote, "A friend, hearing this story, commented that the Dalai Lama might be one of the few people on Earth who has longed for fruitcake." I want His Holiness to know that he is not alone in this longing. But honesty compels me to note that this is the only way in which my life parallels his.

Necessity being the mother of invention, it struck me that contemplation didn't depend on a particular practice. All forms of contemplation share the same goal: to help us see through the deceptions of self and world in order to get in touch with what Howard Thurman called "the sound of the genuine" within us and around us.[1] Contemplation does not need to be defined in terms of particular practices, such as meditation, yoga, tai chi, or *lectio divina.* Instead, it can be defined by its function: *contemplation is any way one has of penetrating illusion and touching reality.*

That definition opened my eyes to myriad ways I might lead a contemplative life—as long as I keep trying to turn experience into insight. For example, facing into failure can help vaporize the illusions that keep me from seeing reality. When I succeed at something, I don't spend much time wondering what I might learn from it. Instead, I congratulate myself on how clever I am, fortifying one of my favorite illusions in the process.

But when failure bursts my ego-balloon, I spend long hours trying to understand what went wrong, often learning (or relearning) that the "what" is within me. Failure gives me a chance to touch hard truths about myself and my relation to the world that I evade when I'm basking in the glow of success and the illusions it breeds. Failure is one of the many forms contemplation can take.

Life is full of challenges that can turn us into contemplatives. Years ago, I met Maureen, a single mother with a daughter named Rebecca who had severe developmental disabilities and could do very little for herself. So Maureen had to live two lives, leaving her with neither time nor energy to go on retreat or take up formal spiritual practices. And yet Maureen was a world-class contemplative.

In her love for Rebecca—who would never be "successful" or "useful" or "beautiful" by conventional standards—Maureen had penetrated every cruel illusion our culture harbors about what makes a human being worthy. She had touched the reality that Rebecca was of profound value in and of herself, a being precious to the earth and a cherished child of God, as everyone is.

To be in Maureen's presence was to feel yourself held in a contemplative circle of grace. When you are with someone who values you not for what you do but for who you are, there's no need to pretend or wear a mask. You experience the blessed relief that comes from needing to be nothing other than your unguarded and unvarnished self.

Even the most devastating experience can be a doorway to contemplation. At least, that's been true for me in the wake of my depressions. While you are down there, reality disappears. Everything is illusion foisted on you by the self-destructive "voice of depression," the voice that keeps telling you you are a waste of space, the world is a torture chamber, and nothing short of death can give you peace. But as you emerge, problems become manageable again, and everyday realities—a crimson glow on the horizon, a friend's love, a stranger's kindness, another precious day of life—present themselves as the treasures they truly are.

If contemplation is about penetrating illusion and touching reality, why do we commiserate with others when they tell us about an experience that's "disillusioned" them?

"Oh, I'm so sorry," we'll say. "Please, let me comfort you." Surely it would be better to say, "Congratulations! You've lost another illusion, which takes you a step closer to the solid ground of reality. Please, let me help disillusion you even further."

I envy people who have whatever it takes to practice classic contemplative disciplines day in and day out—practices that help them get beyond the smoke and mirrors and see the truth about themselves and the world. I call these people "contemplatives by intention," and some I've known seem to be able to get ahead of the train wreck. But I'm not a member of that blessed band.

I'm a "contemplative by catastrophe." My wake-up calls generally come after the wreck has happened and I'm trying to dig my way out of the debris. I do not recommend this path as a conscious choice. But if you, dear reader, have a story similar to mine, I come as the bearer of glad tidings. Catastrophe, too, can be a contemplative path, pitched and perilous as it may be.

I'm still on that path, and daily I stay alert for the disillusionment that will reveal the next thing I need to know about myself and/or the world. Life can always be counted on to send *something* my way—who knows what it will be today? Maybe a reminder of a part of my past that I regret. Maybe a spot on critique of something I thought I'd done well. Maybe a fresh political outrage that makes me feel that my country has lost all semblance of soul.

Whatever it is, I'll try to work my way through it until a hopeful reality is revealed on the other side. Regret can be turned into blessing. Criticism can refocus our work or strengthen our resolve. When we feel certain that the human soul is no longer at work in the world, it's time to make sure that *ours* is visible to someone, somewhere. Those are some of the fruits that can come from being a contemplative by catastrophe.

And never forget that a few slices of bourbon-soaked Trappist fruitcake can help contemplation along.

A Friendship, a Love, a Rescue

> I stand among you as one who offers a small message of hope, that first, there are always people who dare to seek on the margin of society, who are not dependent on social acceptance, not dependent on social routine, and prefer a kind of free-floating existence under a state of risk. And among these people, if they are faithful to their own calling, to their own vocation, and to their own message from God, communication on the deepest level is possible. And the deepest level of communication is not communication, but communion. It is wordless. It is beyond words, and it is beyond speech and beyond concept.
>
> —THOMAS MERTON[2]

I met Thomas Merton a year after he died. I met him through his writing and through the communion that lies

This is an edited version of an essay that originally appeared in *We Are Already One: Thomas Merton's Message of Hope—Reflections in Honor of His Centenary (1915–2015)* (Louisville, KY: Fons Vitae Press, 2015), pp. 24–29.

"beyond words," met him in the seamless way good friends meet again after a long time apart. Without Merton's friendship and the hope it has given me over the past forty-five years, I'm not sure I could have kept faith with my vocation, even as imperfectly as I have.

My vocational journey to what Merton calls "the margin of society"—at least, the margin of my known world—began in 1969 when I was completing my doctoral work at the University of California, Berkeley. As the 1960s unfolded, the academic calling that brought me to graduate school had become less and less audible. Vietnam, a spate of assassinations, race riots and "the fire next time" in several major American cities—all of this had me hearing an insistent inner voice saying, "Your vocation is in the community, not the classroom."

With my PhD in hand, I turned down several opportunities to become a professor, and in July 1969 moved with my wife and children to Washington, DC, to begin work as a community organizer. No one could understand what I was doing, beyond committing professional suicide. In truth, I could not explain it to myself, except to say that it was something I "couldn't *not* do," despite the clear odds against success.

I had no training or experience as a community organizer; much of the work had to be funded by grants that I had no track record at raising; and I was an idealistic and thin-skinned young man temperamentally unsuited for the hard-nosed world of community organizing. Compared to accepting a salaried and secure faculty post, as such posts were back in the day, I was stepping off the edge into "a kind of free-floating existence under a state of risk." Companions would have been comforting, but few are to be found when you go over the cliff.

Meeting Merton

After five months in DC—when the thrill of my free fall had been replaced by the predictable bruises, cuts, and broken bones—I walked into a used book store near Dupont Circle. A friend had recommended that I read *The Magic Mountain* by Thomas Mann. It was not on the shelf, but in the place where it would have been was a book I knew nothing about: *The Seven Storey Mountain* by Thomas Merton.[3] I remember thinking, "It's about a mountain. The author's surname begins with M. That's close enough." So I bought it.

That was early in December 1969. Merton, I soon learned, had died almost exactly one year earlier. But as I read his autobiography, he came alive for me, as he had for millions of readers who'd never met him. I didn't feel that I'd merely discovered a new author worth reading. Instead, I felt I'd met a kindred spirit who understood me better than I understood myself, a fellow traveler who could accompany me on the strange path I had chosen. Or had it chosen me?

Wanting to learn more about my new friend, I set out to read everything he wrote. As Merton devotees know, this would become a lifetime project. The man published at least seventy books, and that counts only those published while he was alive—I've lost count of how many more have been published since his death. I believe his posthumous literary output is the first known case of "perish and publish."

A few years after I began reading Merton, I learned about his correspondence with Louis Massignon, a French scholar who introduced Western readers to the life and work of al-Hallaj, a ninth-century Muslim mystic. Massignon felt that his relation to al-Hallaj was not so much that of a scholar to his subject as it was "a friendship, a love, a rescue."[4] He did not mean that he had rescued al-Hallaj from historical obscurity, but that the Muslim mystic had reached out across time to rescue him.

That's what Merton did for me as I read and reread *The Seven Storey Mountain.* I'm still reading him almost fifty years later, still finding friendship, love, and rescue—essential elements in serving as a messenger of hope. Imparting hope to others has nothing to do with exhorting or cheering them on. It has everything to do with relationships that honor the soul, encourage the heart, inspire the mind, quicken the step, and heal the wounds we suffer along the way.

For nearly half a century, Merton has illumined the path and companioned me on my journey, offering life-giving ways to look at where I've been, where I am, and where I'm headed. Here are a few reflections on four of those ways.

The Quest for True Self

First comes the pivotal distinction Merton makes between "true self" and "false self," which helped me understand why I walked away from the groves of academe toward *terra incognita.* No reasonable person would call my early vocational decisions "smart career moves." But looking at them through Merton's eyes, I came to see that they were first steps in a lifelong effort to be responsive to the imperatives of true self, the source of that inner voice that kept saying, "You can't *not* do this."

I grew up in the Methodist Church, and I value the gifts that tradition gave me. But at no point on my religious journey—which included religious studies at college, a year at Union Theological Seminary, a PhD in the sociology of religion, and active memberships in several mainline Protestant denominations—was I introduced to the contemplative stream of spirituality that Merton swam in and wrote about.

His notion of the quest for true self eventually led me to Quakerism, with its conviction that "there is that of God in every person." The quest for true self and the quest for God: it's a distinction without a difference, one that not only salvaged my spiritual life but took me deeper into it.

"Most of us," as Merton brilliantly observed, "live lives of self-impersonation."[5] I can't imagine a sadder way to die than with the sense that I never showed up here on earth as my God-given self. If Merton had offered me nothing else, the encouragement to live from true self would be more than enough to call his relation to me "a friendship, a love, a rescue."

The Promise of Paradox

The idea of paradox was central to Merton's spiritual and intellectual life, not merely as a philosophical concept but as a lived reality. Given the many apparent contradictions of my life, nothing Merton wrote brought me closer to him in spirit than the epigraph to *The Sign of Jonas*: "I find myself traveling toward my destiny in the belly of a paradox."[6] It is no accident that my first book was titled *The Promise of Paradox,* and featured a lead essay on Merton.

Merton taught me how important it is to look at life not only through the logical lens of "either-or" but also through the paradoxical lens of "both-and." As the Nobel Prize–winning physicist Neils Bohr said, "The opposite of a correct statement is a false statement. But the opposite of a profound truth may be another profound truth."[7] Thinking paradoxically is key to creativity, which depends on the ability to hold divergent ideas in a way that opens the mind and heart to something new. Living paradoxically is key to personal wholeness, which depends on the ability to embrace one's self-contradictions.

For me, reframing life in terms of paradox became a lifesaver. It helped me understand that three devastating experiences of deep darkness—as dark for me as it was for Jonas inside the belly of that whale—did not negate the light that's also part of who I am. "My God, my God, why have you forsaken me?" was the question I asked time and again as I was plunged into darkness in spite of my light. In response, Merton's lived understanding of paradox came to my rescue: to be whole, I must be able to say that I am both shadow and light.

Paradoxical thinking can also save us from the crimped and cramped versions of faith that bedevil Christianity and are, at bottom, idolatries that elevate theological abstractions above the living God. Merton—who had a deep appreciation of Taoism, Zen Buddhism, and Sufism—once put this in words so fierce and forceful that, if taken seriously, would transform the Christian world:

> The Cross is the sign of contradiction—destroying the seriousness of the Law, of the Empire, of the armies . . . But the magicians keep turning the cross to their own purposes. Yes, it is for them too a sign of contradiction: the awful blasphemy of the religious magician who makes the cross contradict mercy! This is of course the ultimate temptation of Christianity! To say that Christ has locked all the doors, has given one answer, settled everything and departed, leaving all life enclosed in the frightful consistency of a system outside of which there is seriousness and damnation, inside of which there is the intolerable flippancy of the saved—while nowhere is there any place left for the mystery of the freedom of divine mercy which alone is truly serious, and worthy of being taken seriously.[8]

The Call to Community

Following the 1948 publication of *The Seven Storey Mountain,* the Abbey of Gethsemani was flooded with young men who wanted to join Merton in the monastic life. Though I was twenty years late to the party, and Merton was no longer with us, I wanted what they wanted. But, as I've said, I had some liabilities when it came to becoming a monk, including a family and Quakerish tendencies. If I were ever to live full-time in a spiritual community, I needed to find another way.

In 1974, I left my community organizing job in Washington, DC, and moved with my family to a Quaker living-learning community called Pendle Hill, located near Philadelphia. For the next eleven years, I shared a daily round of worship, study, work, social outreach, and communal meals with some seventy people in a spiritually grounded community that was as close as I could get to my image of Merton's monastic life. I saw the monastery as a "community of solitudes," a way of "being alone together," a way of life in which a group of people could live more fully into Rilke's definition of love: "that two [or more] solitudes border, protect and salute one another."[9]

This is not the place to write about the many ways a decade-plus at Pendle Hill deepened and strengthened my sense of vocation, a topic I have explored elsewhere.[10] Suffice it to say that in the Quaker tradition I found a way to join the inner journey with social concerns, which later led me to found the Center for Courage & Renewal, an international nonprofit whose mission is to help people in various walks of life "rejoin soul and role."[11] My experience at Pendle Hill also led me to take one more step toward "the margin of society." Since leaving that community in 1985, I've made most of my living by working independently as a writer, teacher, and activist.

When my courage to work at the margins wavers, I take heart in what Merton said in his final talk, given to an international conference of monks in Bangkok a few hours before he died. Quoting a Tibetan lama who was forced to flee his monastery and his homeland, Merton advised the monks, "From now on, Brother, everybody stands on his own feet."[12]

In words that ring true for me at a time in history when our major social institutions—political, economic, and religious—are profoundly dysfunctional, Merton goes on to say:

> [W]e can no longer rely on being supported by structures that may be destroyed at any moment by a political power or a political force. You cannot rely on structures. They are good and they should help us, and we should do the best we can with them. But they may be taken away, and if everything is taken away, what do you do next?[13]

The "Hidden Wholeness" in a Broken World

As the Nigerian novelist Chinua Achebe famously reminded us, "things fall apart."[14] But in "Hagia Sophia," one of Merton's most lyrical meditations, he writes about the "hidden wholeness" the spiritual eye can discern beneath the broken surface of things—whether it's a broken political system, a broken relationship, or a broken heart:

> There is in all visible things an invisible fecundity, a dimmed light, a meek namelessness, a hidden wholeness. This mysterious Unity and Integrity is Wisdom, the Mother of all, *Natura naturans.*[15]

These words, too, have served as a source of hope for me. Once one has eyes to see it, wholeness can always be found, hidden beneath the broken surface of things. This is more than a soothing notion. It's an insight that can shape what the Buddhists call "right action," if we have eyes to see.

Here's an example of what I mean. In the early 1970s—as I was reading Merton and learning a bit about how to organize for racial justice in a rapidly changing neighborhood—I began to understand that my job was not to try to force people into things they did not want to do, such as protesting against unscrupulous real estate practices like blockbusting and redlining. Instead, I needed to give them excuses and permissions to do things they really wanted to do—things related to the justice agenda—but were too shy or fearful to do under their own steam.

For example, the people in the neighborhood where I lived and worked had already run from "the stranger" once, driven by the fears that animate white flight. But in their heart of hearts, they had come to understand that there was no place left to run, no place to escape the diversity of the human community, and that embracing it might bring them peace and enrich their lives.

I knew that step one in stopping real estate practices that manipulate fear to generate profit was simple: give the old-timers and the newcomers frequent chances to meet face-to-face so they could learn that "the other" came bearing blessings, not threats. But instead of asking folks to do the impossible—for example, "Just knock on a stranger's door and get to know whoever answers"—my colleagues and I began creating activities and settings for natural interactions: door-to-door surveys, block parties, ethnic food fairs, and a program we called Living Room Conversations about shared interests, to name a few.

Amid the tensions of "otherness" that are always with us, we helped people act on their deep-down desire to live in the "connectedness" that the human spirit yearns for. And it worked. Over time, because of our efforts and those of many others, a community that might have been shattered became diverse and more whole.

Things do not always work out so well, of course. History is full of tragically failed visions of possibility, and the more profound the vision, the more likely we are to fall short of achieving it. But even here, Merton has a word of hope for us, a paradoxical word, of course:

> [D]o not depend on the hope of results . . . [Y]ou may have to face the fact that your work will be apparently worthless and even achieve no result at all, if not perhaps results opposite to what you expect. As you get used to this idea, you start more and more to concentrate not on the results, but on the value, the rightness, the truth of the work itself.[16]

As long as we're wedded to results, we'll take on smaller and smaller tasks, the only ones that yield results. If we want to live by values like love, truth, and justice—values that will never be fully achieved—"faithfulness" is the only standard that will do. When I die, I won't be asking about the bottom line. I'll be asking if I was faithful to my gifts, to the needs I saw around me, and to the ways I engaged those needs with my gifts—faithful, that is, to the value, rightness, and truth of offering the world the best I had, as best I could.

For helping me understand this—and for imbuing me with the faith that, despite my many flaws, I might be able to live this way—I owe a debt of deep gratitude to Thomas Merton, friend, fellow traveler, and messenger of hope.

Down Is the Way to Well-Being

When I was in my forties, struggling to survive a bout with depression, my therapist said, "You seem to image what's happening to you as the hand of an enemy trying to crush you. Would it be possible to image it instead as the hand of a friend pressing you down to ground on which it's safe to stand?"*

My first thought was, "I need a new therapist." When you're depressed, it seems insulting, even insane for someone to suggest that the soul-sucking Spawn of Satan who has

---

*Depression is a complex topic. I'm qualified to write only about my own experience of it, at least the parts I understand. What I say about it in this book is not meant to apply to all depressions, let alone serve as a "prescription." My focus is on the situational elements of my depression, though it seems likely that elements of brain chemistry and genetics were also involved. People sometimes ask if I'm "for or against" antidepressants. In all three of my depressions, I was on meds for six to twelve months in order to get some ground under my feet, but some people need to be on them for life. I'm for whatever brings genuine relief from misery and allows us to live our lives as fully as we can.

sunk its teeth into you is your BFF. And yet, as time went by, the image of depression as a befriending force began to work on me, slowly reframing my misery and helping me reclaim my mental health. Something in me knew that my therapist spoke the truth: *down* is the way to well-being.

During my first forty years, I'd been driven by the notion that "Up, up and away" was the right direction to go. I had worked hard to achieve altitude because . . . Well, because higher is better than lower, right? Wrong. Living at altitude is dangerous. When we fall, as we regularly do, we have a long way to fall, and the fall may kill us. But a life on the ground—a life grounded in the reality of our own nature and our right relationship to the world—allows us to stumble and fall, get back up, brush ourselves off, and take next steps without doing ourselves great harm.

The altitude at which I was living came from my misuse of four human capacities that, when *rightly* used, can serve us well:

- **Intellect.** As an academic, I'd been trained not simply to think, a capacity I value, but to live mostly in my head, the part of the body farthest from the ground. Learning to think with my mind descended into my heart—integrating what I knew intellectually with what I knew experientially—was not part of the program.[17]
- **Ego.** We all need ego strength, a viable sense of self. But I'd been borne aloft on an inflated ego—an ego that led me to think more of myself than was healthy in order to mask my neurotic fear that I was less than I should have been.

- **Spirituality.** The spiritual yearning to connect with the largeness of life can powerfully enhance one's experience. But the spirituality I'd embraced was more about flying above life's mess than engaging with it on the ground. How did the Christian tradition in which I was raised—one centered on "the Word made flesh"—become so disembodied?
- **Ethics.** I'd tried to live by the precepts of an impossibly out-of-reach ethic—an ethic framed by other people's images of who I *ought* to be and what I *ought* to do. What I needed was honest insight into what is true, possible, and life-giving for *me,* just as I am, broken places and all.

Those external "oughts" had long been a driving force in my life. When I failed to live *up* to them—see how often "up" sneaks into our talk about the good life?—I judged myself as weak and faithless. I was stuck in that stage of moral development where one has high aspirations and equally high levels of guilt about falling short. It's a formula for the good life, I tell you: aim high, hit low, and feel lousy about yourself as you go.

As I took on various issues and causes, I never stopped to ask, "Does such-and-such fit my sense of who I am?" Or "Is such-and-such truly my gift and my calling?" As a result, important parts of the life I was living *were not mine to live,* and thus were bound to fail. Depression was, indeed, the hand of a friend trying to press me down to ground on which it was safe to stand—the ground of my own being, with its messy mix of limits and potentials, liabilities and assets, darkness and light.

Eventually, I developed an image that helped me understand how depression can have a "befriending" intent—and how my failure to "listen to my life" had left me in a place of deep pain. Imagine that for many years a friend had been walking a block behind me, calling my name, trying to get my attention because he wanted to tell me some hard but healing truths about myself. But I—afraid of what I might hear, or arrogantly certain I had nothing to learn—ignored his calls and kept on walking.

So my friend came closer and called my name louder, but I walked on, refusing to turn around. Closer still he came, now shouting my name. Frustrated by my lack of response, he began to throw stones and hit me with sticks, still wanting nothing more than to get my attention. But despite my pain, I kept walking away.

Since calls and shouts, sticks and stones, had failed to get my attention, there was only one thing left for my friend to do: drop the boulder called depression on me. He did it not with intent to kill but in a last-ditch effort to get me to turn toward him and ask a simple question: "What do you want?"

When I finally made that turn—and began taking in and acting on the self-knowledge he'd been waiting to offer me—I was able to take my first steps on the path to well-being.

Thomas Merton's name for that friend is "true self." This is not the ego self that wants to inflate us. It's not the intellectual self that wants to hover above life's mess with logical but ungrounded ideas. It's not the ethical self that wants to live by someone else's "oughts." It's not the spiritual self that wants to fly nonstop to heaven.

True self is the self with which we arrive on earth, the self that simply wants us to be who we were born to be. True self tells us who we are, where we are planted in the ecosystem of life, what "right action" looks like for us, and how we can grow more fully into our own potentials.

As an old Hasidic tale reminds us, our mission is to live into the shape of true self, not the shape of someone else's life:

> Before he died, Rabbi Zusya said: "In the world to come they will not ask me, 'Why were you not Moses?' They will ask me, 'Why were you not Zusya?'"[18]

Memo to myself: stay on the ground, turn around, ask, and listen. True self is true friend—it's a friendship we ignore at our peril. And pass the word: friends don't let friends live at altitude.

Notes from a Week in the Winter Woods

Monday, January 11

Arrived in midafternoon at my rented cabin in the snow-covered Wisconsin countryside. Went inside, lit a fire, and unpacked the car, quickly, motivated by the subzero wind-chill. Outside, acres of bright fields and dark woods. Inside, just me. Plus enough clothing, food, and books—body and soul sustenance for a week of silence and solitude.

Every year, I take a weeklong solitary winter retreat. These are excerpts from a journal I kept during a mid-January retreat in 2016.

Yesterday, as I was packing, a friend asked if I liked being alone. "It depends on who shows up," I said. "Sometimes I'm my best friend, sometimes my worst enemy. I'll see who's there when I get to the cabin."

It's 9:00 p.m., an hour before Quaker midnight, but I'm going to turn in anyway. I'm drowsy and at peace. The fire I've been staring into seems to have burned away the worries that tagged along with me.

Tuesday, January 12

Woke up about 5:00 a.m. and lay awake for another hour in the dark, watching some of my dark emotions rise phoenix-like from the ashes of the night and flap around to get my attention. "Welcome and entertain them all!" says Rumi in his poem "The Guest House." "Be grateful for whoever comes, / because each has been sent / as a guide from beyond."[19]

Guess I need to have a chat with "the beyond." Looks like he/she/it didn't get the memo that I came here for some peace.

Now, a few hours later, I'm feeling that peace again. It came from a breakfast of bacon, eggs, and toast, all ready simultaneously despite the fact that I'm a certified kitchen klutz. My peace came as well from looking out on the snowfields, brilliant under the rising sun and beautifully etched with the shadows of trees and stubble poking up through the snow.

Rumi's "beyond" was right: peace comes from embracing the interplay of shadow and light, and a good breakfast doesn't hurt. After eating, I read the January 12 entry in *A Year with Thomas Merton,* a collection of daily meditations:

> It seems to me that I have greater peace . . . when I am not "trying to be contemplative," or trying to be anything special, but simply orienting my life fully and completely towards what seems to be required of a man like me at a time like this.[20]

Simple and true, that, but so easily lost in Type A spiritual striving. What was required of me this morning was simply to make breakfast, despite my well-documented ineptitude. The deal is to do whatever's needful and within reach, no matter how ordinary or whether I'm likely to do it well.

This afternoon, what I needed was a hike, though the windchill was six below zero. I'm no Ernest Shackleton, but as a longtime resident of the Upper Midwest, I learned long ago that winter will drive you crazy until you get out into it—and I mean "winter" both literally and metaphorically.

"In the depths of winter," said Camus, "I finally learned that within me there lay an invincible summer."[21] I didn't discover summer on my hike. But the sun blazed bright on the frozen prairie, warming my face. And high in the cobalt-blue sky, a hawk "making lazy circles in the sky" as I've seen them do in July. For January in Wisconsin, that's close enough to summer for me.

Wednesday, January 13

I slept poorly last night, and I know why. An hour before bedtime, I binge-ate a box of Jujyfruits while reading a book about spiritual discipline. The book made a few good points but was not well written, and I scarfed down the Jujyfruits as a stimulus to stick with it. My bad, but clear evidence that I could use some discipline.

I feel better now because the oatmeal I made for breakfast—on my second try—was healing. Pure comfort food. On the first try, I got the ratio of oatmeal to water wrong and left it on the burner too long. The pan looked like an avant-garde sculpture of metal fused with grain: *Agrarian Culture in the Machine Age.* Again, my bad, but my kitchen klutz credentials have been fully restored.

I guess my theme today is "Screw-ups in Solitude." In solitude, my bads make me grin. If I committed them in front of others, I'd be embarrassed or angry with myself. Self-acceptance is easier when no one is around.

The Taoist master Chuang Tzu tells about a man crossing a river when an empty skiff slams into his. The man does not become angry, as he would if there was a boatman in the other skiff. So, says Chuang Tzu, "Empty your own boat as you cross the river of the world."[22]

In solitude, I can empty my boat. Can I do it when I'm in the company of other people? Maybe:

> Solitude does not necessarily mean living apart from others; rather, it means never living apart from one's self. It is not about the absence of other people—it is about being fully present to ourselves, whether or not we are with others.[23]

That quote comes from a book I wrote, so I should probably give it a try.

Thursday, January 14

Woke up at 2:00 a.m. and found myself regretting some things I got wrong over the past seventy-seven years. Wished I had been kinder, or braver, or less self-centered than I was, and had a hard time naming the things I got right.

Remembering that the 2:00 a.m. mind is almost always deranged, I finally got up at 4:00 a.m., dressed, made some coffee, stood out into the dark and cold for a bit, and saw Venus gleaming low in the southeast. The goddess of love: that helped.

Then I read the January 14 entry in *A Year with Thomas Merton*. Once again, my old friend had a word I needed to hear, as he reflected on the complex mix of rights and wrongs in his own life: "I am thrown into contradiction: to realize [this] is mercy, to accept it is love, and to help others do the same is compassion."[24]

Merton goes on to say that the contradictions in our lives are engines of creativity. It's true. If we got everything right or everything wrong, there'd be none of the divine discontent *or* the sense of possibility that animates our growth. What we get wrong makes us reach for something better. What we get right reassures us that the "better" is sometimes within our reach.

Memo to self: Remember that you are never in your right mind at 2:00 a.m. Get outside and air out your brain as often as possible. Look for love in all the right places. (Venus isn't a bad place to start.) When all else fails, make coffee.

Now I'm going to take a nap.

Friday, January 15

This morning, for no apparent reason, I woke up with a grin, another one of those "guests" Rumi spoke about, "sent as a guide from beyond." But this time the guest is a welcome lightness, a sense of impending laughter.

Most of my heroes are no strangers to laughter. Grandpa Palmer comes quickly to mind. The man was proof-positive of William James's claim that "common sense and a sense of humor are the same thing, moving at different speeds."[25]

I remember the driving lesson he gave me when I was fourteen, and how I made a dumb, dangerous move on a back-country Iowa road and missed a stop sign. We came to a quivering stop in the middle of a crossroad that could well have had traffic, and Grandpa was ominously silent for a bit. Then he said, laconically, "If I'd of knowed you was gonna do that, I don't believe I'd of asked you to drive." He never said another word about my near disaster, and for the past sixty-three years I've driven accident-free.

Merton was well known for his sense of humor, a quality not uncommon among monks. In *The Sign of Jonas,* a deeply moving journal of his early years in the monastery, there's a line that always makes me smile: "I had a pious thought, but I am not going to write it down."[26]

And I love this claim, found in a Hindu epic called *The Ramayana,* as told by Aubrey Menen:

> There are three things which are real: God, human folly and laughter. The first two are beyond our comprehension, so we must do what we can with the third.[27]

I'm sure I'll experience all three today. The first is ever available, if my heart is open. The second is guaranteed, since wherever I go, there I am. As for the third, laughing at myself can easily consume a couple of hours a day, no problem.

Saturday, January 16

Today's opening line in *A Year with Thomas Merton*: "You can make your life what you want" if you don't "drive [yourself] on with illusory demands."[28] I don't think it's entirely true that I can make my life what I want. But it would help if I stopped making demands on myself that distort who I really am and what I'm really called to do.

After five days of silence and solitude, I'm noticing that many of the demands that hung over me when I came out here have lightened or wafted away. Since I've done little this week to meet those demands, the lesson seems clear: they were mostly the inventions of an agitated mind. Now that my mind has quieted, its tyranny has been undermined, and I feel more at peace.

I recall a story that my businessman dad told me about how he dealt with pressure. In his office, he had a pedestal desk with five drawers in the right-hand pedestal. He'd put today's mail in the bottom drawer, after moving yesterday's mail up to the next drawer, and so on. He'd open letters only after they had made it to the top drawer. By that time, he said, half of the problems people had written him about had taken care of themselves, and the other half were less daunting than they would have been if he'd read the letters the moment they arrived.

True story? I'm not sure—Dad was fond of morality tales. But as Black Elk said to the children in his tribe when he told a teaching story, "Whether it happened that way, I do not know. But if you think about it, you will see that it is true."[29]

Of course, the blessed curse called email did not exist in Dad's day. Still, his story points the way: make five folders for my email, and use them as Dad said he used his desk drawers. In certain respects, I guess you *can* make the life you want.

Sunday, January 17

On this last full day of my retreat, I'm still meditating on the opening line of the January 13 entry in *A Year with Thomas Merton*: "There is one thing I must do here at my woodshed hermitage . . . and that is to prepare for my death. But that means a preparation in gentleness."[30]

What a great leap—from death to gentleness. So different from Dylan Thomas's famous advice to "Rage, rage against the dying of the light."[31] When I was thirty-five, raging seemed right. But at seventy-seven, it's Thomas Merton, not Dylan Thomas, who speaks to me.

The prospect of death—heightened by winter's dark and cold, by solitude, silence, and age—makes it clear that my calling is to be gentle with the many expressions of life, old and new, that must be handled with care if they are to survive and thrive, and that includes me.

Sometimes, of course, that means becoming fierce in confronting the enemies of gentleness around me and within me. If that's a contradiction, so be it. I think Thomas Merton would approve.

Welcome Home

Alone in the alien, snow-blown woods,
moving hard to stay warm in zero weather,
I stop on a rise to catch my breath as the
sun, setting through bare-boned trees,
falls upon my face, fierce and full of life.

Breathing easy now, breathing with the earth,
I suddenly feel accepted—feel myself stand
my own ground, strong, deep-rooted as a tree—
while time and all these troubles disappear.

And when (who knows how long?) I move
on down the trail and find my ancient burdens
returning, I stop once more to say *No* to them—
Not here, Not now, Not ever again—reclaiming
the welcome home the woods have given me.

—Parker J. Palmer

IV. Work and Vocation

Writing a Life

Introduction

I began working at age thirteen as a "landscape architect." For three long, hot summers, I mowed lawns. But I moved up in the world by working as a caddy, public beach house maintenance man, research assistant, community organizer, consultant, professor, dean, writer, founder of a nonprofit, and workshop and retreat leader. And yet, naming the jobs by which I've made a living is not the same as naming the vocation by which I've made meaning.

The way I've earned my keep has changed frequently, but my vocation has remained the same: I'm a teacher-and-learner, a vocation I've pursued through thick and thin in every era of my life. Even when I was cleaning restrooms at a public beach, I was learning a lot about the human condition—mostly things I didn't want to know! But my vocation has found its clearest expression in writing, which I did for many years without compensation.

As we grow older, it's important to get clear about the difference between a job and a vocation. Too many older folks, especially men, fall into despair when their jobs end, because they lose not only their primary source of income (and often have to pick up part-time and poorly paid work) but their sense of identity as well. They had a job to make their living, but they didn't have a vocation to make meaning of their lives, the kind of vocation a person can pursue to the end.

My grandfather, Jesse Palmer, was a machine-tool operator who crafted parts for John Deere tractors. When he was forced to retire at age sixty-five, it was hard for him to say goodbye to his work at the machine shop and his easy camaraderie with colleagues. But Grandpa's vocation was not making tractor parts—it was a love of turning raw material into things of use or beauty, and he pursued it passionately following his retirement.

When he died, I inherited a tiny May basket and a tiny monkey that he'd carved from peach pits, an especially difficult material to work. They sit on a shelf next to my writing desk as a reminder that I can keep using words to carve meaning out of madness long after my writing ceases to be gainful employment.

The opening essay in this chapter, "The Accidental Author," is about how my first book came to be. As the first person in my family to go to college, my idea of publishing a book seemed well beyond my reach. But that did not stop me from following my calling, animated by the passion I felt simply to write. So when the "accident" happened, I had the makings of a book—and I haven't stopped writing since.

"Born Baffled" is about the birthright gift that's animated my writing from the get-go. I'm not an expert on much, but I'm curious, easily confused, even lost, and often in need of finding a way through and out. Writing has been my primary way of puzzling out one bafflement in order to plunge into the next.

"The Poem I Would Have Writ" is about my failed quest to write a book I felt sure I was called to write, a quest I had to lay down after two years of starts and stops. But that quest yielded a five-stanza poem that says all I wanted to say, proving either that I'm a slow learner or that no quest earnestly pursued goes unfulfilled.

"Begin Again" is about the fact that I'm not really a writer: I'm a rewriter who throws away many pages for every one he keeps. This is not only the story of my writing but also the story of my life. More often than I like to admit, I've forgotten lessons learned and had to start over from scratch, relearning what I thought I knew. One advantage of age is the chance it gives us to learn and relearn until we truly know.

"The World Once Green Again" is a poem that reflects the feeling I have when I'm deep into "writing a life"—that my words grow from the seedbed of my experience, just as trees grow from the earth, then return to the earth to "feed the roots of worlds unsung."

If you wonder what my life as a writer has to do with aging, I see powerful parallels between composing sentences, paragraphs, essays, and books and "composing a life," to quote Mary Catherine Bateson.[1] As I say later in this chapter, "With every move we make . . . we're dictating the next few lines of the text called our lives, composing it as we go." How we "write our lives" matters, and with each step we take toward death, our capacity to edit the lives we've written matters even more.

The Accidental Author

Every now and then, someone asks me for advice on how to become a writer. If I'm on my game, I don't offer advice. Instead, I ask questions in hopes of evoking my conversation partner's inner teacher, the most reliable source of guidance anyone has. If he or she presses me, the best I can do is to tell part of the story of my own life as a writer, letting the questioner decide whether there's anything in it for him or her. Call it "advice lite."

The urge to write visited me in my early twenties, and it soon became clear that it was here to stay. Nearly two decades passed before my first book was published, yet I never stopped writing. My daemon would not let me go, nor has it to this day. But, truth be told, that first book had as much to do with happenstance as it did with being daemon driven.

In fall 1978, I taught a class about Thomas Merton. For our final session, I'd planned to show a film of Merton's last talk, given in Bangkok an hour or two before the tragic accident that ended his life. At the last moment, I learned that the 16 mm film I'd ordered—a reel-to-reel movie that required a projector—had been mailed to the wrong address. (No, young people, you couldn't stream or download videos in the olden days, and movies weren't available on DVDs.)

Wanting to bring the class to a proper close, I burned the kerosene lantern late into the night and wrote a lecture to replace the film. One of my students liked the lecture, and asked for a copy to send to her uncle, a Merton devotee. A few weeks later he called me, identifying himself as an editor at a small publishing house. He, too, liked my piece, and wondered if I'd let them publish it in their monthly newsletter. Of course I said yes, feeling as if I'd won the lottery even though no money changed hands.

Two months later, he called again. "Our readers liked your essay," he said. "Have you written others on related topics?" Knowing that I had twenty years' worth of rejected writing interred in my file cabinet, I replied, "I might be able to dig up a few things." "Send them along," he said. So I relit the lantern, spent much of that night exhuming my files, and mailed off a dozen pieces the next day.

A few weeks later, the editor called for the third time. He'd chosen seven or eight essays on the theme of paradox, and wanted to bring them together in a book. "Would that be OK with you?" he asked. I said, "Give me a little time to think about it," swallowed hard and said, "You bet!"

I did some editing to string the pieces together, and wrote some new material to give them a context. Nine months later, I was holding a copy of my first book, *The Promise of Paradox,* gazing at it with a bit of the wide-eyed wonder I'd felt when I held my first child.

Today—thirty-eight years and nine books after that sweet moment—the writing scene has changed, big-time.

I've never had an agent, never self-published, and never had to worry about the reach of my online "platform." But here are three truths from my own experience that still apply.

First, you need to figure out whether your chief aim is to *write* or to *publish*. Two decades of rejection letters would have shut me down if I hadn't decided early on that my primary goal was not to be published but to be a writer—a person who, as someone sagely observed, is distinguished by the fact that he or she writes. Once it became clear that I wanted to write even if the publishing fairy never left a contract under my pillow, I could declare success as long as I kept writing. That's a doable goal, and it's under my control.

Second, you need to chase after dumb luck. When people think I'm joking, I remind them of a simple truth: the more often you get "out there" with your writing— even in a venue as small as a fifteen-student course on Thomas Merton—the more likely it is that dumb luck will strike. So become Jenny or Johnny Appleseed, scattering your words hither and yon, and a few may fall on fertile ground.

But here's the deal: this often means giving your work away when you're getting started as a writer. In addition to being its own reward, this kind of generosity maximizes the chance of dumb luck by giving you more exposure than you get if you try to monetize everything. (And if you want to be respected as a writer, never, ever use words like "monetize." Seriously.)

Third, and most important, allow yourself to be mys-tified, which shouldn't be hard to do. I mean, what's *not* bewildering about ourselves, other people, and the world we share? The problem is that some of us (read "the person writing this sentence") sometimes make the mistake of writing in an effort to pretend we're smarter than we are.

Take my early writing . . . please! When I go back and read some of that schlock, I don't know whether to laugh or cry as I watch this pitiful fellow slogging through page after page of multisyllabic muck, making his case with "academic rigor" and nary a drop of uncertainty, playfulness, or humanity. What I regarded as rigor was actually rigor mortis.

I was writing to impress rather than express, always a bad idea. I was trying to persuade my readers that I was an expert on my subject, rather than a guy trying to understand things that feel like bottomless mysteries to me—teaching, social change, spirituality, democracy, and so much more. My best writing originates not in expertise but in a place called "beginner's mind."

For me, writing is not about gathering facts, wrapping them in lucid thoughts, then getting them down on the page. It begins with dropping deep into my not-knowing, and dwelling in the dark long enough that my eyes adjust and start to see what's down there. I want to make my own discoveries, think my own thoughts, and feel my own feelings before I learn what the experts say about the subject.

Novices are often advised, "write about what you know." I wouldn't call that bad counsel, but I'd extend it a bit: "Write about what you *want* to know because it intrigues and puzzles you." That's the hunger that keeps me engaged with a craft I find endlessly challenging, of which sportswriter Red Smith said, "There's nothing at all to writing. All you do is sit down at a typewriter and open a vein."[2]

Evocative questions are almost always more helpful than advice. But for whatever it's worth, my "advice lite" boils down to this: (1) Care more about the process than the outcome. (2) As you are getting started, give your work away in order to maximize the chances of dumb luck—and keep giving it away whenever you feel so moved. (3) Be willing to dive deep, spend a long time floundering, and practice beginner's mind no matter how loudly your ego protests.

Come to think of it, the same counsel might apply to things other than writing. Hmmm, maybe there's a new book in that . . .

Born Baffled

When I agreed to speak at a conference on faith and writing, my timing was off. A month before the conference, I might have had uplifting things to say about writing, and I might have had some faith. But when the date arrived, the book I was working on had me stuck in one of the sub-basements of hell.

Down there they practice reverse alchemy: the golden words I write in the early morning turn to dross by lunchtime. When they do, the kindest thing I can say about writing is to quote that cheery fellow, George Orwell:

This is an edited version of a talk I gave on April 17, 2010, at Calvin College's annual Festival of Faith & Writing.

Writing a book is a horrible, exhausting struggle, like a long bout of some painful illness. One would never undertake such a thing if one were not driven on by some demon whom one can neither resist nor understand.[3]

For over fifty years, I've invited that demon into my life time and time again, well aware that illness will follow. The only known cure is to finish the piece I'm writing before it finishes me—to wrestle it to the ground the way Jacob wrestled the angel—until the misery gives way to something that feels like grace. Here's a place where faith and writing converge: no matter which path you're on, it's often hard to tell whether you're wrestling with angels or demons.

But I'm not complaining. I love the challenge of writing and the feeling of aliveness it brings me, even when the flames start licking at my feet. As Mark Twain said, "Go to Heaven for the weather, Hell for the company."[4]

As a grade schooler, I was convinced that my whole purpose in life was to become a pilot. I wanted nothing more than to "slip the surly bonds of earth / and dance the skies on laughter-silvered wings."[5] So I spent a lot of time building, flying, and often crashing model airplanes, as many boys did back in the day.

But unlike most of my friends, I spent even more time making small pamphlets about how airplanes do what they do. I "published" them on folded, stapled paper filled with carefully typed words, accompanied by illustrations on such topics as how the curve of an airfoil creates lift as the engines draw the plane through the air. Clearly, what I *really* wanted when I was young was to be not a pilot but a writer. I wanted to write books about life's mysteries—such as how very heavy objects manage to stay aloft with no visible means of support.

Years ago, someone asked me why I became a writer. I'd been asked before and had given various bogus responses because I didn't know the answer. But this time, I nailed it: "I became a writer because I was born baffled."

Here's another thing faith and writing have in common. Like writing, faith is a way of dealing with things that baffle us until we look at them through new eyes. "By faith we understand that the . . . visible has its origin in the invisible" (Hebrews 11:3), as does the magic that makes a Boeing 777 climb into thin air.

Bafflement is, I believe, one of my birthright gifts. I must have emerged from the womb, been slapped into breathing, taken a look around and said, "What the heck is this all about?" Born into a world where there's a lot that's baffling, I never lack for subjects. So my approach to writing is simple: I find something that baffles me, write enough to peel back the first layer of my not-knowing—at which point I find another bafflement, then another, and keep writing until I've gone as far as I can, certain that eventually I'll find another layer of mystery beneath the last one I explored.

Here's a short list of the kinds of things that baffle me:

- Why do so many affluent Americans who have more money and material goods than they need never feel that they have enough?

- Why do so many well-educated people understand precisely how the material world works, but are clueless about their own inner dynamics?
- Why do some citizens say they love democracy, but constantly put it at risk with name-calling, fear-mongering, and ruthless scapegoating?
- What's with me, this guy who's so aware of what's baffling about others, but sometimes finds himself believing one thing, saying another, and doing yet another?

Fueled by the contradictions within and around me, I spend a lot of time writing about them, not least those found in my own faith tradition. What's going on when a tradition founded on "the Word become flesh" is so fearful of the body and sexuality? Or when a tradition grounded in "love your neighbor" makes so many neighbors into the fearsome "other" and casts them into the outer darkness?

Some folks seem to think that questions of this sort are inimical to faith. But faith is what allows us to live in full awareness of our contradictions—an awareness that breeds the humility that's part and parcel of true faith. For me, it's faithless to be so afraid of the contradictions in ourselves and our religious communities that we have to pretend there aren't any.

In fact, to believe that our spiritual lives are without contradictions is worse than faithless. It gives rise to the kind of arrogance that allows some of my coreligionists to play leading roles in the evils of racism, misogyny, homophobia, and xenophobia—even as they proclaim that every human being is created in God's image.

In my experience there is only one way to make myself, my faith, and my world appear to be consistent and coherent: fake it. I don't normally speak for God, but I'm quite sure that the God of reality does not favor fakery—which, among other things, keeps us from confronting our own need for transformation.

❧ ❧ ❧

Speaking of fakery, one of the great temptations of being a writer is to absorb the projections of readers who think you're an expert on some subject just because you've written a book about it. When I was young, my ego often became bloated with those projections. I forgot the counsel my father gave me when I was a kid: "Remember, Park, today's peacock is tomorrow's feather duster."

When my ego becomes bloated with the illusion of expertise, I risk losing the gift of bafflement that has always animated my best writing. I stop asking questions and start believing I have answers. In an effort to preserve my gift, I've tried to write candidly about my limitations, flaws, failures, and shadows. When I'm able to do that honestly and well, it helps the reader see me not as an expert but as who I am: a fellow traveler, a companion on the life journey.

I've never felt obliged to share the whole of my brokenness in public. As a Jungian therapist once told me, "The soul needs its secrets." Only when I've thoroughly integrated a hard experience into my sense of self can I tell my story in a way that makes safe space for the reader to reflect on his or her hard times. It took me ten years following my first descent into deep darkness before I could write about it without causing the reader to worry about my well-being.

Nothing has been more satisfying for me as a writer than the gratitude I've received from fellow sufferers for what I've written about clinical depression. Yet I've never been able to write as if I knew what people who suffer as I have ought to do to find their way through. Books about "tips, tricks, and techniques" tend to leave me cold; telling your story truly and well is more than enough for me. When you share your story of struggle, you offer me companionship in mine, and that's the most powerful soul medicine I know.

Here, it seems to me, is yet another parallel between faith and writing. The God I'm familiar with does not work like a GPS, but accompanies me as I try to grope my way through the darkest of dark places. I think a good writer can do at least a little bit of that for the reader; writing from a deeply human place of vulnerability is an act of compassion, as well as self-therapy.

And yet, for all the importance I attach to telling parts of my shadow story, there's a personal downside to it. As soon as I put the story on paper, it begins to become stylized, fixed, and frozen. The original experience loses vitality as I put it into words and those words get published. Tell the story often enough, and it stops being a soul story and starts becoming a shtick, especially if it draws an affirmative reaction from readers.

When I write or speak such stories, it's tempting to say to myself, "As long as it's essentially true and reaches people, who cares if it's a caricature of your experience?" Well, my soul cares. It doesn't like it one little bit when I distort its experience. When I do, the life-giving power and meaning of that experience will fade for me in direct proportion to the distortions in the story I tell.

Truth, says Barry Lopez, cannot "be reduced to aphorisms or formulas. It is something alive and unpronounceable. Story creates an atmosphere in which it becomes discernible as a pattern."[6] When a story tells the truth, that pattern is almost as ephemeral as a pattern made by the wind in prairie grass. If you tell the story too literally, to make sure the reader "gets it," the pattern looks less like wind in the grass and more like stakes hammered into the ground.

As a writer who wants to touch his readers by making a soul connection on the printed page, I have a dilemma. Do I tell my soul story in a way that readers will find clear and compelling, staking it out as I go? Do I hint at it with the impermanence of the wind telling tales in the grass? Or do I withhold the story altogether in order to preserve its truth and freshness for myself? The answer, I suppose, is "It depends."

What's clear is that writing is a kind of public therapy for me—which carries an obligation to remember that parts of my therapy must be confined to trusted friends or a professional. As the nineteenth-century English actress Mrs. Patrick Campbell said of overly intimate public displays of affection, "I don't care what they do, so long as they don't do it in the street and frighten the horses."[7]

Since writing is sometimes a form of prayer for me, here's another parallel between faith and writing: "When you pray, do not be like the hypocrites, for they love to pray standing . . . on the street corners to be seen by men . . . When you pray, go into your room, and close the door" (Matthew 6:5). Or, as Mrs. Patrick Campbell might say, "When you pray, don't frighten the horses."

⁓ ⁓ ⁓

Writing is a *retrospective* act that helps me sort, sift, and come to terms with my own experience. But it's also a *prospective* act, a Distant Early Warning system about the next opportunity or demand for new growth I need to attend to. Looking back, I realize that every book I've written was preparing me for what was to come next, though I did not know it at the time—though at age seventy-nine, I'm sure that writing a book about aging with mortality in mind is an act of preparation!

When I write, I seem to be partnering with something that is not yet me or mine—or perhaps with something more truly me than I normally have access to. Many of us, said Thomas Merton, live lives of "self-impersonation."[8] Writing allows my mask to fall away so my true face can appear and I can get a clearer look at things I need to be facing into.

My first book was *The Promise of Paradox: A Celebration of Contradictions in the Christian Life.* In it, I was trying to learn how to hold my own contradictions with the help of a concept that ultimately became central to all my work: paradox, the notion that life's most important realities often take the form of both-ands rather than either-ors.

The darkness that overtook me a year or two after writing *Promise* came from a longtime habit of ignoring my shadow side, and one of the most valuable assets I had during that perilous time was the concept of paradox. Paradox helped me embrace the fact that I'm both a good guy and a bad guy, that life is forever a dance of darkness and light, and that the mystery some call God contains the same duality: "I am the Lord thy God who makes weal and creates woe" (Isaiah 45:7).

Promise was primarily an inward-looking book. But it got me reflecting on the way our inner and outer lives continually merge into each other, cocreating us and the world as they do. I came to call this phenomenon "life on the Möbius strip." So my second book—*The Company of Strangers: Christians and the Renewal of America's Public Life*—took me from the inner surface of that Möbius strip to the outer. Once again, writing prepared me for where I needed to go before I got there.

In *Company,* I was trying to map a spiritual journey that does not lead to narcissism, a condition worsened by the belief that God dwells only in the hidden heart. I was seeking ways to integrate spirituality with our calling to help cocreate a world of love and justice. I needed to write about life in "the company of strangers" to keep from ending up in a gated spiritual community of one.

Having written about the inner life in my first book, and the public life in my second, I needed to face the fact that I am neither a full-time monk nor a full-time political activist. One way or another, I'm a teacher, no more and no less. Whether I'm working in a classroom, facilitating a retreat, organizing a project or a community, or sitting in solitude writing, I'm a teacher at heart.

So in books three and five—*To Know as We Are Known: A Spirituality of Education* and *The Courage to Teach: Exploring the Inner Landscape of a Teacher's Life*—I found myself exploring my vocation as a teacher. I was trying to understand how teaching relates to the inner and outer life questions that occupied me in books one and two. I emerged with more clarity about how to bring both contemplation and action into "the teaching life."

None of my books was animated by the thought, "I know where life is taking me, so I need to write my way there." In each of them, I was simply trying to peel off layers from some of my bafflements. Only in retrospect am I able to say that I wrote my way toward my growing edge before I had even a glimmer of where it might be.

〜 〜 〜

The German novelist Thomas Mann said that "a writer is someone for whom writing is more difficult than it is for other people."[9] In truth, it's so difficult for me that I can't honestly call myself a writer: I'm a rewriter. I toss out a dozen pages for every one I keep, and I don't think I've ever published anything short of a seventh or eighth draft.

My incessant rewriting is not driven by perfectionism, whose grip I shook off a long time ago. Every time I rewrite a piece, I'm driven by curiosity: What lies around the next bend of the road in this convoluted world, or in my own convoluted mind?

I'm often surprised by what I discover, and by the sense that it had been sitting there waiting for me to find it. This explains why, time after time, when someone cites a few lines from one of my books, I'll ask myself, "Did I really write that?" I barely recognize it as my own thought because, in one sense, it isn't. It's an insight I stumbled across on my way to who-knows-where.

Here's a question at the heart of both writing and faith: As we explore reality with words or leaps of faith, are we discovering or inventing our findings? My best guess is that the answer is "Yes." That answer is important not only because I think it is true but also because I believe it can help keep us humble about our convictions.

What does it mean to say that something is both a discovery and an invention? When I was a kid, we had fun taking a piece of paper and writing messages on it with a thin brush dipped in lemon juice. When the juice dried, the page looked blank. But when we held the paper over a source of heat, the words we had written would magically appear.

These days when I write—at least, when it's going well—I have a sense that the words I choose to put on paper are intersecting with realities that are already "out there," but will remain invisible until someone gives them verbal form. When it's not going well, what's happening is the converse: I'm using words to try to force something into being, to "reveal" something that's not really there— or I've not yet found words with the power to make reality show up on the page.

So when my writing isn't going well, which happens a lot, I must be willing to commit "conceptual suicide" again and again. I must tear up the pages I've labored over for hours, days, or weeks, and start over from scratch if what

I've written, no matter how elegant, is not tapping into truth. It's as if I were a kid again, holding a piece of paper over a source of heat, but no hidden messages are emerging on the page.

For a happy marriage between reality and words, reality must be honored with words that reveal its nature. Even the simplest realities won't reveal themselves if you use the wrong words—and even words that seem right won't reveal things that aren't there. As with any marriage, we try to meet in the middle, in "the place just right." Then we fall away from that place and have to work to get back there again.

My incessant rewriting is evidence that I often fall away. But I'm willing to commit conceptual suicide as often as necessary to get to a place where my words can have a live encounter with reality.

At this point, my parallel journeys as a writer and person of faith come together as one. For many years, a passage from the New Testament has commanded my attention: "We have this treasure in earthen vessels to show that the transcendent power belongs to God and not to us" (II Corinthians 4:7).

In religious terms, the treasure is God; in secular terms, it's reality. The earthen vessels are (among other things) the words we choose to convey what we know and believe. For me, the meaning of the verse is simple yet demanding: every vessel we create to hold the treasure is earthen, finite, and flawed, and is never, ever to be confused with the treasure itself.

Writers are in the business of crafting earthen vessels to hold what we've found in our inquiries into reality. If our clay pots prove too cramped to hold the treasure well, if they keep us from having a live encounter with what's true—or if they prove so deformed that they defile rather than honor the treasure they are meant to hold—then we must smash them and find something better suited to holding the treasure and passing it along.

Smashing clay pots is called iconoclasm, a good thing when it's needed. The failure to do it when needed is called idolatry, always a bad thing. In both writing and faith, we need to commit conceptual suicide again and again—if we are serious about the vastness of the treasure and the inadequacy of our frail, finite, and flawed words.

When people of any tradition insist that the treasure cannot be carried except in *their* earthen vessels, they commit idolatry, and sometimes people die: idolatry is the driver behind all religious violence. Why do we do it? Because we are afraid—afraid of how we'd have to change if we freed the sacred from our creedal cages and released it back into the wild.

Of course, we can never confine the sacred, but the delusion that we can dies hard. I once heard an old Celtic Christian story about a monk who died and was interred in the monastery wall. Three days later, the community heard noises inside the crypt, so they removed the stone and found their brother resurrected. Awash in wonder, they asked him what heaven was like. "Well," he said, "it's nothing at all like the way our theology says it is . . ."

Without further ado, they put him back in the wall and sealed the crypt again.

For me, the constant challenge of both faith and writing is to hold the paradox of the treasure and the earthen vessel with deepest respect. The vessels deserve our respect because they give us a chance to protect the treasure, share it with one another, and pass it along to the next generation. But if a vessel begins to obscure the treasure, we must toss it into history's landfill in favor of one that reveals more than it conceals.

Failing to do that, we fail the treasure, which does not belong to us: we belong to it. To deny or defy that fact is the ultimate disrespect. It leads not to life but to death, for individuals, religious communities, and the world.

On the bulletin board over my desk, typed on an index card yellowed by time, I keep a quote from the Spanish writer José Ortega y Gasset:

> Why write if this overly-easy activity of pushing a pen across paper is not given a certain bullfighting risk, and we fail to take on dangerous, agile and two-horned topics?[10]

And why have faith, if God is so small as to be contained within our finite words and formulae? To write and live in faith, we must let God be God —original, wild, free, a creative impulse that animates all of life, but can never be confined to what we think, say, and do. Thank God for that!

The Poem I Would Have Writ

Our lives leave a trail of words, even when we're not speaking or writing. With every move we make—at home and at work, with friends and with strangers, in public and in solitude—we're dictating the next few lines of the text called our lives, composing it as we go.

How best to go about "composing a life"? That's the title of a fine book by Mary Catherine Bateson, so I know I'm not alone with my question.[11] Wordsworth said we arrive on this planet "trailing clouds of glory."[12] What kind of text trails behind us as we live out our time on earth? Does it read as tedious or banal, uncaring or resentful, fearful or angry, or something better by far than any of that?

Fifty years ago, when I was in my late twenties, lost and seeking guidance on what it means to live well, I found a compelling clue to composing "something better" in Henry David Thoreau's *A Week on the Concord and Merrimack Rivers.*

In a prose passage on a life in art—without explanation or elaboration, as if the idea had just popped into his head and he had to capture it before it fled—Thoreau drops this simple couplet:

My life has been the poem I would have writ
But I could not both live and utter it.[13]

What a remarkable notion, that the text one writes with one's life might be a poem! Of course, if you regard poetry as little more than flowery verse, you'll find the idea cloying: life is not all sweetness and light. But neither is poetry, rightly understood. The poet Paul Engle says, "Poetry is boned with ideas, nerved and blooded with emotions, all held together by the delicate, tough skin of words."[14] And Robert Penn Warren adds, "For what is a poem but a hazardous attempt at self-understanding: it is the deepest part of autobiography."[15] Poetry at its best is as close to the bone as life itself.

Thoreau's claim that we can live our lives as a poem seized my youthful imagination. As time went by, his couplet began to haunt me, or taunt me. I sensed that it held a secret I only half understood. So in my mid-seventies, I set out to discover that secret by trying to write a book titled, of course, *The Poem I Would Have Writ.*

I reread Thoreau, collected quotes and footnotes, made outlines and sketches, wrote and rewrote chapters, and talked with my friends about it until they must have wished I'd get a new idea. Or new friends. After an ungodly amount of research, reflection, and writing, it became clear that my book just wasn't going to happen. I abandoned the project, laid low by the failure of my longtime quest.

But here's the thing about the fact that we are all dictating words with our lives: keep living and the words keep coming. Pay attention to what they say, and occasionally they will surprise you by composing themselves into something of meaning.

One day, as I sat down for my early-morning journaling, Thoreau's couplet came back to me for the umpteenth time—that's how obsessions work. Thirty minutes later, a poem had shown up in rough draft, and after playing with it for a few more days, I felt I'd come as close as I could to the secret of "the poem I would have writ."

It took me fifty years of being dogged by Thoreau's couplet to arrive at this destination—not a book of many pages, but a five-stanza poem written by an amateur who loves to watch life become words and words become life. That's one stanza per decade.

Still, the journey is the destination, and I've learned from every step. With this poem in hand, praise be, I can finally make peace with the book that will never be, the book I thought I should have writ.

The Poem I Would Have Writ

My life has been the poem I would have writ
But I could not both live and utter it.

—HENRY DAVID THOREAU

The first words are the hardest.
Sound surrounds you in the womb,
grows louder when you're born.
You listen, for the day will come
when you must speak words, too—
that's how we make our way
thru this trackless landscape
called the world. But how?
And what to say? And what
does saying do?

Later, words come easily. You learn
to speak the language of what you
want and need, to help you find a
pathway into and through your life,
to make it clear what you believe,
reach out to friends, find work to do,
heal your wounds, ease your fears,
get chance on chance to give love
and receive. Sometimes words leap
out of you in ways you soon regret—
or in ways so magical you silently
rehearse them, hoping never to forget
how they came out of the blue,
demanding to have life
breathed into them by you.

Then you learn that first words aren't
the hardest. The hardest are the last.

There's so much you want to say,
but time keeps taking time and all your
words away. How to say—amid the
flood of grief and gratitude you feel—
"Thank you!," or "How beautiful, how
grand!," or "I don't know how I survived,"
or "I was changed forever the day
we two joined lives and hands."

As you reach for your last words,
you realize, this is it—this ebbing tide
of language called your life, words
trailing into silence, returning to
the source—this unfinished poem
you would have writ, had it not been
for the heartache and the joy
of all the years you've been living it.

—PARKER J. PALMER

Begin Again

Not long ago, I saw *Begin Again,* a film starring Keira
Knightley and Mark Ruffalo that tells a tale about love and
music set on New York's Lower East Side.

I hung out in that neighborhood occasionally in the
early 1960s, drawn at age twenty-two to the hipsters,
artists, and *philosophes* who populated the area. I was in
New York to study for the ministry at Union Theological
Seminary, but I sensed that my divinity gig might fall
through. So it seemed prudent to cultivate—how shall I
say?—a philosophical fallback position. I guess I thought
that drinking espresso and breathing the East Village air
would make an existentialist of me.

Begin Again spoke to me for several reasons, not least
that I got a good laugh out of remembering who I was in
my early twenties. But this isn't a movie review or a mini
memoir. It's a meditation on the film's title, and how those
two words help me get "unstuck."

I've been feeling stuck about many things, including how to respond to the world's nonstop saga of suffering: the ongoing carnage in the Middle East, the endless episodes of mass killings in the United States and around the world, the racism deep in the DNA of my native land, our collective blind eye to radical economic injustice and climate change, and the grotesque parade of grandstanding political "leaders" who bloviate about God and prayer while doing squat about gun violence and other evils.

I've also been feeling stuck as a writer, having recently watched a book die at my keyboard. Forgive me for adding a trivial personal problem to my list of major social ills, but we all live at the intersection of our small worlds and the big one around us. If we want to serve others, we must attend to both. Since writing is one of my main ways of making meaning, writer's block is a vexing problem for me.

Like most of us, I have other ways of making meaning, of course. I sit with folks who want to explore their problems or pursue their dreams. I lead renewal retreats for people in the serving professions. I've been assisting my granddaughter with a project on homelessness. I also help out at home as allowed, which means doing tasks that don't involve food prep and/or breakable things.

Still, I've been feeling sidelined by my inability to get traction with my writing. Friends have advised me to think of this as a fallow period, a time to let the soil renew itself before I try to grow a new crop. Well, I've had fallow times, and they felt life-giving. Being stuck has felt more like stagnation, and whether you're eighty or eighteen, there's no life in that.

The day after I watched *Begin Again,* the movie's title came back to me in the form of guidance: *You need to begin again.* I don't mean begin again with a new book. I mean begin again with what Buddhists call "beginner's mind."

Then I recalled a poem that now reads as if it were written to help me find a way forward. Here's Wendell Berry's tribute to his old friend, the celebrated poet Hayden Carruth, who was in his eighties when Berry greeted him "at the beginning of a great career":

To Hayden Carruth

Dear Hayden, when I read your book I was aching
in head, back, heart, and mind, and aching
with your aches added to my own, and yet for joy
I read on without stopping, made eager
by your true mastery, wit, sorrow, and joy,
each made true by the others. My reading done,
I swear I am feeling better. Here in Port Royal
I take off my hat to you up there in Munnsville
in your great dignity of being necessary. I swear
it appears to me you're one of the rare fellows
who may finally amount to something. What shall
I say? I greet you at the beginning of a great career?
No. I greet you at the beginning, for we are
either beginning or we are dead. And let us have
no careers, lest one day we be found dead in them.
I greet you at the beginning that you have made
authentically in your art, again and again.[16]

To get unstuck, I must let go of my "career" as an established writer and begin again as a novice. In truth, I *am* a novice in every new moment of the day—each of them presents possibilities unknown and untried. Why not embrace that fact and see what happens? As Zen teacher Shunryu Suzuki said, "In the beginner's mind there are many possibilities, in the expert's mind there are few."[17]

What does it mean in practical terms to begin again? I was afraid you'd ask. The truth is, I'm clueless—which may prove, *mirabile dictu,* that I'm actually practicing beginner's mind. If I'd waited for an answer, I wouldn't have written this little piece—and writing it may help me get unstuck as a person, as a writer, as a citizen of the world. Simply pecking away at it over the past few days has already made me feel less stagnant and more alive.

Of course, nothing I eventually write or do will solve those urgent problems I named. But since writing is one of my main ways of engaging the world, whatever I write will help me get reconnected and might even move me toward other ways of being useful.

I doubt that I'm the only one who has been feeling stuck. If you're another, let's remind each other that the planet cries for all of us to contribute our personal gifts—whatever they may be—to the common good. Let's make a pact of mutual support to begin again with beginner's mind and with hope.

The World Once Green Again

That tree from its dense wooden trunk
surprises into leaf
as my tight-fibered heart leafs out
in unexpected speech.

I know that trunk, that heartwood core,
dark and dense, so like my own.
Yet here I celebrate that we
can take leave of our density
to dance the wind and sing the sun.

Our words, like leaves, in season spring
and then in season fall,
but at their rise they prove a power
that gentle conquers all.

As shriveled leaves return to earth
to nourish roots of leaves unsprung,
so dry words fall back to the heart
to decompose into their parts
and feed the roots of worlds unsung.

And when speech fails, the dark trunk stands
'til most surprising spring
wells up the voice that ever speaks
the world once green again.

—Parker J. Palmer

V. Keep Reaching Out
Staying Engaged with the World

Introduction

In 1974, when my family and I moved to the Quaker living-learning community called Pendle Hill, I knew only a little about Quaker faith and practice. Hoping to learn more, I attended a large annual gathering of Friends at the historic Arch Street Friends Meeting House in Philadelphia.

As I walked into the growing crowd, I noticed half a dozen elderly women chatting with each other. Every one of them had her white hair tied up in a bun, the way my grandmother wore hers. I smiled and thought to myself, "How sweet to have memories of Grandma rekindled! I can even catch a faint scent of the apple pie that often filled the kitchen of her simple home . . ."

In the midst of my reverie, one of the women looked my way, broke off from the group, and walked directly to me. Without any preliminaries, she grabbed my arm as if to keep me from fleeing, and said, "I've just returned from a meeting in Des Moines about Native American rights, and I want to tell you what I learned"—which she did, in considerable detail, as she tried to recruit me for her project.

When she left, having achieved her goal, I thought, "She's not Grandma and apple pie! She's the kind of person I want to be when I'm an old man!"

Our youth-oriented culture sends a message to elders that can discourage and defeat us: "It's time to withdraw from serious engagement with a world that's changing so rapidly you can't possibly keep up. So take up harmless hobbies and hang out at home."

There are only three problems with this message: (1) It robs older folks of sources of vitality, meaning, and purpose. (2) It robs the world of the gifts elders have to offer. (3) It's ridiculous. Other than that, it's a great idea.

When I'm with elders whose world has shrunk to the dimensions of their TV room—and who have no health problems to limit their mobility—it's as if I'm with the walking dead. But when I'm with elders who have a mind-and-heart connection with the world beyond their walls, I find their vitality contagious, even if they are confined to their homes.

I'm lucky to have the capacity to continue to live an active life. But the essays in this chapter have nothing to do with volunteering for local projects, marching in protests, or going to Washington, DC, to lobby Congress, as much as I applaud all that. Instead, they reflect the way we can stay engaged with public life by using our voices and speaking our minds. If publishing an essay or a book isn't your thing, you can write letters to the editor, speak up at local forums, or talk with family and friends about things that matter to you and to them.

"Keep reaching out" means saying to the world, "I'm still a member of this community. I have a voice and things I need to say, and I want to be part of the conversation." Even more important, it means saying all of that to yourself until it's engraved on your heart.

In the first essay, "What's an Angry Quaker to Do?," I ask whether anger has a place in the life of someone who aspires to live nonviolently and yearns for a world of love, peace, and justice, as I do. (Spoiler alert: I conclude that it does.) This essay and others in this chapter are laced with my political convictions. Please understand that I write not to change yours, but to encourage you to express them, as citizens of a democracy have the right and responsibility to do.

"The Soul of a Patriot" was written in response to the fact that, on November 8, 2016, as I worked on this book, my country elected a president who, by any measure I know, from moral to intellectual, is woefully unfit for that job. Worse still, he was catapulted into power by forces, such as white supremacy, that threaten our democracy. To channel my anger and fear in creative directions, I needed to reconsider the meaning of the word *patriot*.

"In Praise of Diversity" makes the case that homogeneity is as dangerous to a society as it is to an ecosystem when it comes to productivity, creativity, sustainability, and resilience. America is headed toward a future in which white people will constitute less than half of our population. Our fear of "otherness"—manipulated by unscrupulous politicians to gain and secure power—will be our undoing, unless "We the People" learn to value our differences and allow our tensions to pull us open to something new rather than pull us apart.

"Seeking Sanctuary" is about finding the solace and support we need when our engagement with the rough-and-tumble world of politics starts to cost us our physical and mental well-being. I explore the variety of forms that sanctuary can take, assisted by the singer-songwriter Carrie Newcomer, whose music is itself a form of sanctuary.

"The Winter Woods" is a meditation on the beauty and grace that lie just beneath the brokenness of our world. Looking at the shattered surface of our common life can send us into despair. Seeing the wholeness beneath the shards can encourage us to keep reaching deep for something better—something that's already there, hidden in plain sight.

What's an Angry Quaker to Do?

> Return to the most human, nothing less
> Will nourish the torn spirit, the bewildered heart,
> The angry mind: and from the ultimate duress,
> Pierced with the breath of anguish, speak for love.
>
> —MAY SARTON, "SANTOS: NEW MEXICO" (EXCERPT)[1]

I'm a Quaker. I stand in a religious tradition that asks me to live by such values as community, equality, simplicity, and nonviolence. As a result, I frequently find myself in deep oatmeal, especially when it comes to politics, where I seem to have an anger management problem. A few years ago, a friend with whom I have "spirited" political discussions gave me a T-shirt that says, "One Mean Quaker."

Does anger have a role to play in the life of someone who aspires to nonviolence? For better or for worse, it's a reality in mine. Exhibit A is the anger I feel toward our forty-fifth president, who, among character defects too numerous to name here, lies with abandon. The man has an astonishing gift for denying having said things that were captured on videotape—and, when the tape is played back, calling it "fake news." As one journalist has said, lying has become "the defining feature" of his presidency.[2]

To add injury to insult, he tells weaponized lies that can harm and even kill people. Those at risk include immigrant parents and children who now must worry about keeping their families intact; Muslims, Jews, people of color, and LGBTQ folks who find themselves in the crosshairs once again; people whose longtime jobs in coal mines and factories will not be resurrected; and democracy itself, which dies when we cannot trust our leaders or each other.

So, yes, I'm one angry Quaker when it comes to this president and his people, who keep insisting that the emperor has new clothes, then blame and ban journalists for not telling the world how good he looks in them.

Occasionally, I'm taken to task by people who regard anger as a spiritual flaw to be eliminated. But I beg to differ:

- When something is morally wrong, so is ignoring it in homage to the Gospel of Nice. If I weren't angry about the lies so brazenly scattered about by this administration, and the cruelties they encourage, I'd fear that I am as unprincipled as they are.
- I'm all for forgiveness as an antidote for anger, and I believe Anne Lamott's line that "not forgiving is like drinking rat poison and waiting for the rat to die."[3] But forgiveness, I've discovered, is not always mine to give, especially in relation to people who have long histories of malicious acts and see no need to seek forgiveness. Sometimes I have to pass the forgiveness baton to higher powers, as Iris DeMent does in her tragicomic country and western song: "God may forgive you, but I won't. Jesus may love you, but I don't."[4]
- I know that anger has the potential to harm the person who's angry, and others in his or her orbit. But I also know that anger buried under a pious cover poses more threats to my well-being—and that of those around me—than anger expressed nonviolently. Repressed anger is dangerous, a weapon we aim at ourselves that sooner or later injures others. But anger harnessed as an energy that animates social action on behalf of new life for all is redemptive.

Before I'm condemned by the "spiritually correct"—whom I find more offensive than their "politically correct" counterparts—please note that my anger is aimed at our forty-fifth president, not at those who voted for him. That's a big change for me, brought about by the inner work I've been doing since Election Day 2016, when I was angry at all his supporters and the horses they rode in on.

Setting aside those for whom I have only contempt—for example, anti-Semites, white supremacists, and wealthy tax-evaders who don't know the meaning of "enough"—I've come to understand that many who voted for this president had reasons related to the economic challenges they face, and the fact that for decades, politicians from both major parties have done little or nothing to help.

The words of the poet May Sarton helped me get started on this journey of empathy for my fellow citizens. The first verse of her poem "Santos: New Mexico" appears at the head of this piece. Here's the last verse, where she describes an alchemy that can transform anger from a death-dealing force into a power for new life:

> Return to the most human, nothing less
> Will teach the angry spirit, the bewildered heart,
> The torn mind, to accept the whole of its duress,
> And pierced with anguish, at last act for love.[5]

What does it mean to "return to the most human" as we try to morph our anger into acts of love? For me, it means returning to my own story in order to reconnect with the stories of those who differ from me politically.

I'm a straight, white, financially secure male, who has benefited from the perks the United States so readily bestows on people like me. I have none of the urgent financial concerns that drove some votes in the last election. The education I've been able to afford—along with the time and inclination I have to read a variety of news sources—has made me less likely to fall for fake news, "alternative facts," and false reasoning. For decades, I've been blessed with a diverse band of colleagues and friends whom I love and respect, so the fear of "the other" that drove voters who have little experience of diversity is not a driver for me.

If I'm unable to understand that my life story gives me good reason—and a few tools—to understand people whose lives and politics differ from mine, then I'm as mindless and heartless as our current leaders.

What does it mean, in the words of May Sarton, to "at last act for love"? For me, it means at least this: I want to redouble my efforts to help us renew our capacity for civic community and civil discourse. I want to harness the energy of anger and ride it into action that helps bring citizens together in life-giving encounters. If the reality of We the People continues to fade into mist and myth, we'll lose our democracy.

So I'll continue with the project I launched in 2011 when I published *Healing the Heart of Democracy,* one that involves helping all of us, myself included, to resist the "divide and conquer" strategy that undermines the reality and power of We the People.[6] This is the work of cultivating civil discourse, a way of talking to each other across our political divides that is less about watching our tongues than valuing our differences.

Only by discussing our differences openly, honestly, and with civility can we honor the intentions of the framers of the Constitution who gave us the first system of government that regards conflict *not as the enemy of a good social order but as the engine of a better social order*—if we hold our conflicts creatively. This work does not have to be done in large-scale public forums, but can and should be done in smaller venues: the family, a friendship, a neighborhood, a congregation.

To keep myself honest, I want to continue to hold the question I asked at the start of this essay: "Does anger have a role to play in the life of someone who aspires to nonviolence?" I want to stay alert to those moments when my anger has no honest origin or worthy destination, and has not been harnessed as energy for something potentially life-giving.

But as I do, I'll take solace from Psalm 58, where a certified holy man angrily petitions God to "smash the teeth" of those who spread poisonous lies (Psalm 58:6). The Psalmist does not recommend direct action of this sort, and neither do I. Radical oral surgery should be left to the Almighty.

And yet, if the Psalmist's petition were to be granted today, I can imagine at least two positive outcomes. The lying would cease for a while since it would be too painful to talk, which seems only fair since it's so painful to listen. And we might get a national health care plan with better dental coverage.

Spirituality and anger (and humor) are not necessarily at odds. Or so it seems to One Mean Quaker as I continue to stumble through life—well aware that, before too long, I'm likely to find myself in deep oatmeal again.

The Soul of a Patriot

I was very young when I first heard about "the soul." For years, I thought of it as a wispy spirit within me, well intentioned but too frail for life's toughest challenges. Then, in my forties, I had my first experience of depression, drawn there partly by genetics and partly by making some bad choices.

During my long months of dwelling in the dark, the powers I depended on—intellect, emotions, ego, and will—proved useless. My mind became my enemy, my feelings went numb, my sense of self was annihilated, my willpower reduced to nil. Every one of my normal supports collapsed under the weight of my life.

But every now and then, I sensed the presence of an original core of self that knows how to persist in hard times, the grounded, gritty life-force that gives "soul music" its name. As my other powers failed me, this core—as savvy and sinewy as a wild animal—helped me survive, then thrive. There's much I don't know about this primal wildness I came to liken to my soul, but I know this: it's unafraid of the dark, it loves life and light, and it tells us the truth about ourselves and how we get lost and might find our way home.

Recently, I've been lost in the dark again. This time, it's a darkness more political than personal, a darkness we *all* helped to create. That includes people like me who were so cocksure that we knew the score that we couldn't be bothered to look, listen, and learn outside our cultural comfort zones.

On January 20, 2017, the country I love inaugurated a president who embodies many of our culture's most soulless traits: adolescent impulsiveness, an unbridled drive for wealth and power, a taste for violence, nonstop narcissism, and massive arrogance. A man who has maligned women, Mexicans, Muslims, African Americans, immigrants, members of the LGBTQ community, people with disabilities, and Mother Earth—a man who'd sooner deny the obvious than apologize for the outrageous—became the putative "leader of the free world."

How do I stay engaged and whole when my country is under attack by an enemy that *we* invited in? When I put that question to my soul, I got an unnerving response. I'm called to become a "patriot," a word I scrapped years ago when it was co-opted by the "God, Guns, Guts, and Glory" gang.

Then a succinct, discerning, and powerful passage on patriotism by pastor/activist William Sloane Coffin—whose work always came from his soul—launched my search for ways to reclaim that word for myself:

> There are three kinds of patriots, two bad, one good. The bad ones are the uncritical lovers and the loveless critics. Good patriots carry on a lover's quarrel with their country, a reflection of God's lover's quarrel with the world.[7]

What would it mean to have a "lover's quarrel" with my country right now, animated by the fierce love for which the soul is famous? So far, I've come up with four responses to that question.

First, it must be a quarrel about what is and is not true. Our forty-fifth president's enablers have proclaimed truth passé. To cite three of them:

> There's no such thing . . . anymore of facts.
> —SCOTTIE NELL HUGHES[8]

> You [journalists take] everything . . . so literally. The American people . . . [understand] that sometimes [like at a bar] you're going to say things [with no] facts to back it up.
> —COREY LEWANDOWSKI[9]

> You [reporters] always want to go by what's come out of his mouth.
> —KELLYANNE CONWAY[10]

We who hold the quaint belief that it's often possible to figure out whether what comes out of a mouth is true or false—and that it's important to do so when the mouth in question is that of the president—need to assert the facts every chance we get.

For example, the president who has claimed that only he can save our economy also claimed that there are "96 million . . . wanting a job [who] can't get [one]." False. There are "roughly 96 million people not in the labor force, but that includes retirees, students and others who [aren't looking for] jobs. Only 5.5 million of them [are seeking] work."[11] And before this man got anywhere near the White House, the unemployment rate—which neared 10 percent during 2010, following the financial meltdown of 2008—went down to 5 percent or less in 2016, due in part to his predecessor's policies.[12]

Facts are so tedious, aren't they? And they won't change the minds of true believers. But we need to preserve them for the same reason medieval monasteries preserved books: the torches have come to town. Let's try to remember that science and the Enlightenment gave us ways to test the truth claims of potentates and prelates, laying the foundations for our experiment in democracy. Until someone blows up the lab, we must proclaim the facts, then secure them in a fireproof vault, until the next time we need them, which probably will be afternoon.

Second, we must engage in civil discourse across political divides, without compromising our convictions. That's been a daunting task to date, it's going to get even harder, and we're not very good at it. But this much is clear: for dialogue to succeed, participants must have *something* in common.

I believe we have all kinds of shared interests. We breathe the same air, use the same roads and bridges, depend on the same institutions, and must find ways to live in harmony for the sake of our children and grandchildren. But appeals to the obvious have yet to bring us together. So my hope lies in a shared condition that isn't yet with us, but eventually will be, I believe.

Our forty-fifth president has a long history of leaving people holding the bag.[13] Sooner or later, some of the people who helped put him in office will realize that he is not going to deliver for them, either because he never intended to or because he lacks the political chops to do so.

At that point, people who were political enemies in 2016 *might* find some common ground, and a Coalition of the Disillusioned *might* become possible. I'm disillusioned by the shell game that took this man to the White House. People who supported him because he promised to bring back lost jobs, revive the middle class, restore law and order, kill ISIS, and "drain the swamp" in Washington, DC, may eventually become disillusioned with him.

When the common ground of "We've been had!" makes dialogue possible, it will give people like me a chance to do what we've failed to do in the past: listen empathetically to the alienation felt by that segment of the president's base who voted for him because they felt unheard. We're now in a better position to understand their sense of diminishment because we feel diminished, too.

Third, this lover's quarrel needs to surface what is *not* being said. This is a form of "telling the truth in love" that's as critical to the health of our civic relationships as it is in our intimate relationships.

Amid all the talk about the "why" of the election results, we've not talked enough about the fact that, by midcentury, over half of US citizens will be people of color.[14] After 250 years, we're at the beginning of the end of white European dominance in this country. It's no coincidence that white votes were key to the 2016 election, nor that white nationalists and white supremacists rallied enthusiastically to the winner's banner, with no real pushback from him.

We're either in the death throes of a culture of white supremacy or resuming our unfinished Civil War. Either way, we who care about the fate of the United States need to work hard to steer these death-dealing energies toward life-giving outcomes.

Finally, if it's going to be a *lover's* quarrel, we need to keep the love alive. Paradoxically, this means remembering that the country we love has forever fallen short of its own values and visions. I can truly love another person only if I don't romanticize him or her, and the same is true of loving my country.

The next time you hear the fanciful notion that we must "Make America Great *Again*," think slavery, the Civil War, Jim Crow, the New Jim Crow, the Great Depression, Vietnam, Joe McCarthy, Iraq, homelessness and hunger, the greed-driven financial meltdown of 2008, and much, much more. Then ask, "Which period of American 'greatness' are we talking about?" Then note how we Americans double down on our illusions by claiming that we are "a shining city upon a hill."

This "post-truth presidency," with all its moral deformations, is nothing new.[15] The country I love is inherently flawed, as are all human constructs and all human beings. That's why our imperfect founders placed the endless task of seeking a "more perfect Union" at the heart of the American agenda.

January 20, 2017, is not when "things fell apart" in the United States. It's one more in a long history of such moments. We've overcome before, and if we love our democracy as fiercely as we should, we can overcome again.

I didn't watch the 2017 inauguration. Instead, I helped lead a weekend retreat for hospital chaplains, people devoted to healing, as millions of Americans are. But at the hour when the country I love was inaugurating a man who does not even vaguely resemble the "better angels of our nature," I was silently reciting a line that has served me well since grade school: "You're not the boss of me."

Those words remind me that among my unalienable rights is the freedom to follow my soul instead of my leaders, if in doing so I serve the common good. They also encourage me to persist in my lover's quarrel with my country, as a patriot must.

In Praise of Diversity

Jean-Paul Sartre famously said, "Hell is other people." I wonder what J-P was doing just before he wrote those words. Enduring a business lunch where the main course was braggadocio? Or an employer-mandated pep talk by a "motivational speaker"? Or any cocktail party, anytime, anywhere? If so, I feel his pain.

But as a generalization, Sartre's definition of hell is a reach too far for me. My hell is much more specific. It's a place populated *exclusively* by straight white males over fifty who have college degrees and financial security—which is to say, people like me. For me, variety is more, much more, than the spice of life. It's a basic ingredient of a life lived fully and well.

At a time when so much of American life is driven by fear of "otherness"—by a false and toxic nostalgia for "the good old days" when "we were all alike"—let's ask where we would be without diversity. What price would we pay if all our companions came from backgrounds akin to our own and looked at life more or less the way we do?

Mother Nature can help us answer that question, as I learned when I visited a friend who lives in rural Minnesota. We took a drive on the back roads, passing acre after acre of corn lined up in orderly, homogeneous, and mind-numbing rows. As we crested a hill, my friend broke the silence: "Check it out."

There, afloat in the sea of uniformity called agribusiness, was an island of wind-blown grasses and wildflowers, a riot of colors and textures to delight the eye. We walked silently through this patch of prairie my friend had helped restore, dotted with the kinds of plants whose names make a "found poem:" wild four o'clock, bastard toadflax, prairie smoke, amethyst shooting star. After a while, my friend spoke again, saying something like this:

> There are more than 150 species of plants on this prairie—to say nothing of the insects, birds, and mammals they attract—just as there were before the pioneers broke the sod and began farming. It's beautiful, of course, but that's not the whole story. Biodiversity makes an ecosystem more creative, productive, adaptive to change, and resilient in the face of stress. The agribusiness land around us provides us with food and fuel. But we pay a very steep price for that kind of monoculture. It saps the earth's vitality and puts the quality and sustainability of our food supply at risk.

The prairie as it once was has a lot to teach us about how we need to live.

The parallels between biodiversity and social diversity seem clear and compelling to me. Here are just a few of them:

1. **Diversity makes our lives more vital.** Regular experiences of "otherness" not only bring blessed relief from the tedium of endlessly recycling the same ideas with the same people. They also dial down the fear of "the other" that keeps us from feeling at home on earth, sapping *our* vitality.

People who wall themselves off from diversity in gated communities and lifestyle enclaves become increasingly paranoid that encountering the other will put them in harm's way. But folks who have daily experience in "the company of strangers" learn that it just isn't so. Up close, it becomes clear that people who don't look and sound like us don't have horns, and some have haloes.

In my late twenties, on vacation in a distant state, I took a hike in the woods while my young family enjoyed the beach at a state park. An hour later, I was hopelessly lost and in a panic, worried about the setting sun and my family's well-being.

I stumbled into a small neighborhood at the edge of the forest and began knocking on doors. Four times I was turned away by people who were clearly afraid of me and my breathless plea for help. At the fifth door, the gentleman said, "Hop into my truck. I'll have you at the beach in five minutes." My Good Samaritan was black; the others were white.

One story does not good sociology make, but I've seen that pattern play out time and time again, driven not by genetics but by social experience. The white folks who turned me away either had never been lost and scared, or were afraid of someone who was. But in America—with its history of slavery, Jim Crow (old and new), and "sundown towns"[16]—people of color learn early in life what lost and scared feels like, and the result can be compassion.

2. **Diversity makes us smarter and more creative.** People from different backgrounds know different things and have different ways of interpreting what they know. As we come together in a "dialogue of differences," the collective becomes smarter than any individual in it. That principle applies to everything from practical problem solving, to scientific inquiry, to speculating on the eternal mysteries: all of us together are smarter than any one of us alone. Ask any high-tech company CEO whose creative teams look like a good day at the United Nations.

Homogeneity dumbs us down and gets us into trouble. I mean the kind of dumb that comes, for example, from knowing so few Mexicans, or so little about them, that we're more likely to fall for the lie told by our forty-fifth president that many of them are drug dealers, rapists, and assorted "bad hombres."[17]

Recently, some Americans have been taking a crash course in the consequences of this kind of dumb. On February 9, 2017, the much-loved manager of a Mexican restaurant in a Midwestern town was "detained" by the US government without notice and taken away from his family and his community. Later that month, one resident who supports the deportation of undocumented immigrants spoke for many:

> [M]aybe this should all be more on a per-case basis. It's hard to be black and white on this because there may be people like Carlos.[18]

Right. But wouldn't it have been keen if this gentleman and his fellow citizens had known enough Mexicans—or had had enough moral imagination—to figure out that whole "black and white" thing before Carlos was deported, his family devastated, and his community deprived of an exemplary citizen who had lived there for a decade?

3. **Diversity gives us a chance to increase our personal resilience,** and God knows some of us need it these days. I'm one of the many weary souls who is still laughing at a line Jon Stewart, late of *The Daily Show,* delivered just eleven days into the administration that shall go unnamed: "The presidency is supposed to age the president, not the public."[19]

During the painful months following the 2017 presidential inauguration, I felt more like Methuselah than a relatively healthy septuagenarian. "Really?" I thought. "Is this the way I'm going to go out, suffering daily from fresh assaults on dignity, decency, democracy, and truth itself that grind down my morale and make me ashamed to be an American?"

I began to recover my resilience as I talked with friends who—along with generations of their ancestors—have been targets of such assaults since the day they were born, yet have refused to be intimidated.

My Muslim, Mexican, and African American brothers and sisters have developed a form of spiritual alchemy that all of us can practice. It transforms the dross of political evil into the gold of political activism, revitalizing us to be the engaged citizens we should have been all along. Resilience comes from seeing people I care about take the next assault on their souls not as a reason to give up but as reason to redouble their efforts.

4. **Diversity ups the odds that we will enjoy the benefits of the human comedy.** Cross-cultural misunderstandings are not always train wrecks. Some of them generate healing and life-giving humor.

I once spoke at a Jewish Community Center built around a beautiful garden dedicated to the memory of Jews who had been murdered in the Holocaust. After sitting quietly there for half an hour, I met with the Center's director and told him how moved I was by this powerful witness to the suffering and the resilience of the Jewish people.

He told me that the Center also tried to witness the importance of interfaith relationships—which meant, among other things, hiring a religiously diverse staff. Then he said,

> Occasionally this leads to some laughable and loveable moments. We recently hired a Gentile as our front-office receptionist. We told her that when we answer the phone, we say, "Jewish Community

Center—Shalom." I happened to be in the office when she took her first phone call and said, "Jewish Community Center—Shazam!"

The goodwill laced through stories like that help fortify my hope that we can emerge from these dangerous days on the diversity front with our humanity intact.

I recently heard an interview with Pat Buchanan, a once-major political figure who has always longed to return America to the days when white, European, Christian culture dominated. Of course, he's delighted with the current administration's "success" in advancing his agenda, and is unfazed by our forty-fifth president's multiple personal flaws and string of political failures.

When the interviewer asked him, in effect, "Why is diversity a problem for this nation?" this three-time presidential aspirant said, "Well, maybe it's preference. I feel more comfortable. I'm a homeboy, and I feel more comfortable with the folks I grew up with."[20]

So there you have it, the personal truth behind much of the high-flying "Make America Great Again" rhetoric. Pat Buchanan and his political pals want this nation to provide them with a homogenous—read "racist and xenophobic"—comfort zone, from sea to shining sea.

Mr. Buchanan is my age, and I know enough sclerotic and scared old white guys like him to feel a subatomic particle of pity. But guys, you need to get with the program: by midcentury, the number of Americans who are of white European descent with be less than 50 percent.[21]

I urge those of you who cling to your dream of the "good old days"—good for *you,* anyway—to take a nice long nap and dream on, dream on. The rest of us will stay awake and help midwife the rebirth of America, hoping that our national nausea in this moment is just another symptom that our country is pregnant with change.

Given careful tending, America can be like that restored prairie my friend showed me, with its rich diversity of life, vitality, creativity, resilience, and soul-satisfying array of textures and colors. Every time I touch in with that memory—or step into that social reality—my mind is renewed, my heart expanded, my spirit refreshed, and I feel at home again on the face of this good earth.

Seeking Sanctuary

When I was a kid, "sanctuary" meant only one thing. It was the big room with the stained glass windows and hard wooden benches where my family worshipped every Sunday. Church attendance was not optional in my family, so that sanctuary was where I learned to pray—to pray that the service would end and God would let my people go. I also learned that not all prayers are answered, no matter how ardent.

Today—after eight decades of life in a world that's both astonishingly beautiful and horrifically cruel—"sanctuary" is as vital as breathing to me. Sometimes I find it in churches, monasteries, and other sites formally designated "sacred." But more often I find it in places sacred to my soul: in the natural world, in the company of a faithful friend, in solitary or shared silence, in the ambience of a good poem or good music.

Sanctuary is wherever I find safe space to regain my bearings, reclaim my soul, heal my wounds, and return to the world as a wounded healer. It's not merely about finding shelter from the storm—it's about spiritual survival and the capacity to carry on. Today, seeking sanctuary is no more optional for me than church attendance was as a child.

We live in a culture of violence. Even if we're not at daily risk of physical injury or death, as so many are in the gun-obsessed United States, our culture relentlessly assaults our souls with noise, frenzy, consumerism, tribalism, homophobia, misogyny, racism, and more. It's common to become desensitized to these assaults. We normalize them in order to get on with our daily lives, disregarding our need for sanctuary as we do. But at times something happens that makes us hypersensitive to all that threatens our souls.

My three bouts with depression were such "somethings" for me. For long months, I lived in closed rooms with the shades pulled down. When a friend told me to get outside more, I said, "I can't. The world feels like it's full of knives."

In my fragile mental state, even casual encounters felt perilous, and overhearing the news of the day made me feel utterly unfit for life in this world. I exaggerated life's dangers and underestimated my own resilience. But recalling the bad old days when my world was all sharp edges reminds me that in a violent culture, it's easy to die the death of a thousand cuts.

People have different ways of dealing with cultural violence. Some turn to escapism by, for example, embracing world-rejecting religious or political beliefs. But this almost always leads to deepening isolation, a siege mentality, and paranoia about how "those people" or "the government" are trying to control us and destroy our way of life. There's a lot of that going around these days.

Others jump into the American mosh pit, seeking wealth or power or notoriety, contributing to the world's violence as they do. There's a lot of *that* going around as well, despite warnings like the one Wordsworth famously issued two hundred years ago:

> The world is too much with us; late and soon,
> Getting and spending, we lay waste our powers:
> Little we see in Nature that is ours;
> We have given our hearts away, a sordid boon![22]

Others try to call our culture back to sanity and make the world a better place. Yet even they can get caught up in the violence of the very culture they want to change: we live in it, and it lives in us. To quote Thomas Merton,

> [T]here is a pervasive form of contemporary violence to which the idealist . . . most easily succumbs: activism and overwork. The rush and pressure of modern life are a form, perhaps the most common form, of its innate violence. To allow oneself to be carried away

by a multitude of conflicting concerns, to surrender
to too many demands, to commit oneself to too many
projects, to want to help everyone in everything is to
succumb to violence. More than that, it is cooperation
in violence. The frenzy of the activist neutralizes his
work . . . It destroys the fruitfulness of his own work,
because it kills the root of inner wisdom which makes
work fruitful.[23]

Merton names one of our deepest needs: to protect
and nurture the "root of inner wisdom" that makes work
and life itself fruitful. Fed by the taproot some call the soul,
we need neither flee from the world nor exploit it. Instead,
we can love the world with all of its (and our) flaws, aspir-
ing to the best of the human possibility.

We can live that way only if we know when and where
to seek sanctuary, reclaiming our souls for the purpose of
loving the world. When service emerges from whatever
nurtures the root of one's inner wisdom, it's much less likely to be distorted by the violence of activism and overwork.
Once we understand that, we are moving toward the heart
of nonviolence—the only way of being that has a chance to
transcend and transform the violence of our culture.

I was reminded of this fact in March 2011, when I
went on the annual three-day Congressional Civil Rights
Pilgrimage led by Rep. John Lewis.[24] On the first day, we
visited movement sites in Birmingham, Alabama; on the
second day, in Montgomery; and on the third day—the
forty-sixth anniversary of "Bloody Sunday"—we marched

across Selma's Edmund Pettus Bridge with John Lewis once again in the lead, as he had been in 1965 at age twenty-five.[25]

During that pilgrimage, two things struck me about the history we revisited. The first was the fact that so many young people had been so well schooled in nonviolence that they were able to sustain ferocious attacks from sworn "public safety" officials without striking back. By refusing to succumb to the violence of our culture, they transformed a struggle that might have become armed warfare into a moral witness that altered the lay and the law of the land.

The second was the fact that most of the civil rights sites we visited were sanctuaries like the one I sat in as a restless kid—sanctuaries in which generations of African Americans planted the seeds of the movement that flowered in the mid-twentieth century. I was especially moved by Brown Chapel AME Church in Selma.[26] That's where peaceful protestors prepared for the first march across the Edmund Pettus Bridge—and sought refuge after being bloodied and broken on the other side.

As a person who aspires to live nonviolently—knowing I will forever fall short—I know I need sanctuary if I want to loosen the grip of our culture's violence on me. I also know that there are many Brown Chapels. The one I need may not be a building, but silence, the woods, a friendship, a poem, or a song.

As I worked on this essay, I had a long talk about it with my friend and colleague Carrie Newcomer. A few weeks later, she sent me a song called "Sanctuary" that she'd written in the wake of our conversation. The song itself has become a place of sanctuary for me. May it serve you that way as well.*

The Winter Woods

The winter woods beside a solemn
river are twice seen—
once as they pierce the brittle air,
once as they dance in grace beneath the stream.

In air these trees stand rough and raw,
branch angular in stark design—
in water shimmer constantly,
disconnect as in a dream,
shadowy but more alive
than what stands stiff and cold before our eyes.

Our eyes at peace are solemn streams
and twice the world itself is seen—
once as it is outside our heads,
hard-frozen now and winter-dead,
once as it undulates and shines
beneath the silent waters of our minds.

When rivers churn or cloud with ice
the world is not seen twice—
yet still is there beneath
the blinded surface of the stream,
livelier and lovelier than we can comprehend
and waiting, always waiting, to be seen.

—PARKER J. PALMER

VI. Keep Reaching In

Staying Engaged with Your Soul

Introduction

Some people don't know what "reaching in" means, despite the fact that for millennia the world's wisdom traditions have majored in mapping various pathways to the soul. The clueless ones are not to blame. From elementary through graduate school, we receive little guidance for the inner journey, even though Socrates—the patron saint of education—regarded self-examination as key to a life worth living.

When we're young and wholly engaged with the external world, we may manage to feel "alive" for a while without an inner life. But when we experience diminishments and defeats—the kind that can come at any age and are inevitable when we get old—we run the risk of feeling dead before our time if we lack inner resources. Yet, not all is lost. As the poet Rilke says:

> You are not dead yet, it's not too late
> To open your depths by plunging into them
> and drink in the life
> that reveals itself quietly there.[1]

What do I mean by an "inner life"? I mean a largely silent, solitary process of reflection that helps us reclaim the "ground of our being" and root ourselves in something larger and truer than our own egos. Only so can we put our lives in perspective, embrace our shadow and our light, transcend the regrets and fears that often come with age, and reconcile ourselves to what the poet Stanley Kunitz calls the heart's "feast of losses."[2]

Of course, the inner journey has its challenges, which is why some of us are loath to take it. When we go inward, we are forced to meet our demons face-to-face, to travel long miles in the dark without being able to see the light at the end of the tunnel.

The challenges and rewards of making that journey have been summed up brilliantly by the writer Annie Dillard:

> In the deeps are the violence and terror of which psychology has warned us. But if you ride these monsters down, if you drop with them farther over the world's rim, you find what our sciences can not locate or name, the substrate, the ocean or matrix or ether which buoys the rest, which gives goodness its power for good, and evil its power for evil, the unified field: our complex and inexplicable caring for each other, and for our life together here. This is given. It is not learned.[3]

If it's true, as I claimed in the Prelude, that old is just another word for nothing left to lose, then taking the risk of a deep inward dive should get easier with age. It's a risk we need to take. Aging and dying well, like everything else worth doing, require practice—practice going over the edge toward "the substrate, the ocean or matrix or ether which buoys the rest."

The first essay in this chapter, "Embracing the Human Frailty," is about learning to welcome everything that's come into our lives—the good, the bad, and the ugly—as teachers with lessons for us. We may scream at the heavens, "In the name of all that is holy, no more learning experiences, please!" And yet, the older we get, the more our lives are enriched by lessons we weren't ready to learn when we were young.

"Confessing My Complicity" is focused on being white in a society rooted in white supremacy. I'm not on a guilt trip here, just acknowledging the inner roots of a social pathology that, if it goes unconfessed and unaddressed, will make people who are like me a continuing part of the problem. No disease in the United States is more in need of a cure than racism—which breeds irrational fears that, in turn, breed the worst of political evils. As long as I draw breath, I want to be part of the solution. That requires a close examination of my own heart and dealing with whatever pathogens I find there. If I want to help heal the world, I must heal myself.

When we leave self-protective delusions behind, and engage consciously with realities like racism and death itself, we often experience the heartbreak we've been trying to protect ourselves against. "Heartbreak and Hope for New Life" is about the transformative power of the heart that's broken *open*, not *apart*. The broken-open heart is a place of spiritual alchemy, where the dross of hard experience can be transformed into the gold of wisdom. All it takes is practice, practice, practice!

"A Season of Paradox" is about what we can learn from autumn, when the falling and dying we see all around us are, in fact, seeding a season of rebirth. Autumn in the natural world reminds us that the "little deaths" we experience in the autumn of our lives, and the "big death" that will happen when we go over the brink, are necessary for new life to emerge.

"Appalachian Autumn" is a poem I wrote during a lovely October afternoon in a Kentucky hollow, or "holler," as folks in Appalachia call it. The ancient mountains around me put my life in perspective, taking me on an inner journey that had no words, until this poem began to come to me.

Embracing the Human Frailty

The Guest House

This being human is a guest house.
Every morning a new arrival.

A joy, a depression, a meanness,
some momentary awareness comes
as an unexpected visitor.

Welcome and entertain them all!
Even if they're a crowd of sorrows,
who violently sweep your house

empty of its furniture,
still, treat each guest honorably.
He may be clearing you out
for some new delight.

The dark thought, the shame, the malice,
meet them at the door laughing,
and invite them in.

Be grateful for whoever comes,
because each has been sent
as a guide from beyond.

—RUMI[4]

The first time I read "The Guest House," I felt certain
that Rumi wrote it especially for me, as if he'd been reading
my journal. It's not uncommon for me to be visited by the
feelings he names—"a depression, a meanness," "the dark
thought, the shame, the malice."

Rumi tells us to open the door to these "unexpected
visitors," but in my experience, that's not necessary. If the
door's not open, they'll blow it off its hinges, or break in
through the windows, or come down the chimney like
Anti-Claus.

Once they're in, I don't want to "welcome and entertain them all" as Rumi advises. Instead, I want to give them
the boot with a line from the painter Walter Sickert, who
once told an annoying guest, "You must come again when
you have less time."[5]

Still, Rumi insists that we should not only welcome these troublesome guests but "be grateful for whoever comes." Even if they "violently sweep your house / empty of its furniture," he says, they may be "clearing you out / for some new delight."

For a long time, I thought Rumi meant, "These hard feelings will pass, and happier ones will take their place." Then it dawned on me that even when the vandals are trashing my guest house, their very presence is a sign that I'm human. As Rumi says, "This being human is a guest house." That fact unites me with everyone who acknowledges and accepts his or her human condition. For me, it is a source of reassurance that we have a lot of company on this endless and sometimes perilous road to becoming more fully human.

Gandhi called his autobiography *The Story of My Experiments with Truth*.[6] Experimentation is how we learn, and a lot of experiments fail. If you live your life experimentally, the failures will be personal, and some will be spectacular. And yet, as every scientist knows, we often learn more from experiments that fail than from those that succeed.

Thomas Merton, Trappist monk, is one of my personal saints even though he's unlikely to be sainted by his own church because of his spectacular "failures" by ecclesiastical standards. Not only did he find wisdom and consolation outside of Christianity in Taoism and Buddhism,[7] but toward the end of his life, Merton fell deeply in love with a nurse who cared for him when he was in the hospital.

During a long, tortured year—when his life became a trashed "guest house"—Merton wrestled with whether to leave the monastery and marry the woman he loved.[8] Ultimately, he made the painful decision to maintain his monastic vows. But one of Merton's close friends told me that, when the pain had eased, Merton said something remarkable about this intimate "experiment with truth": "I finally learned that I'm capable of loving someone other than God."

How amazing that this world-class mystic said, in effect, "Loving God is a piece of cake compared to loving another human being. Being human is harder than being holy." Merton had come to understand what the writer John Middleton Murry meant when he said, "For a good man to realize that it is better to be whole than to be good is to enter on a strait and narrow path compared to which his previous rectitude was flowery license."[9]

This is the demanding path toward wholeness. It's a path that takes us toward being fully human, one that can be walked only by those willing to fall down and get up time and again. And being human, fully human, is something to be celebrated, as Merton did in a journal entry about the epiphany he had in downtown Louisville, Kentucky:

> In Louisville, at the corner of Fourth and Walnut, in the center of the shopping district, I was suddenly overwhelmed with the realization that I loved all those people, that they were mine and I theirs, that we could not be alien to one another even though we were total strangers. It was like waking from a dream of separateness, of spurious self-isolation in a special world, the

world of renunciation and supposed holiness . . . This sense of liberation from an illusory difference was such a relief and such a joy to me that I almost laughed out loud. And I suppose my happiness could have taken form in the words: "Thank God, thank God that I am like other men, that I am only a man among others."[10]

Once, when I took one of my failings to a trusted counselor and friend—a man who knew how to "hear me into speech," to paraphrase theologian Nelle Morton[11]—I was blessed with words I'll never forget: "Welcome to the human race." My friend was not scandalized by the fact that I had fallen. He'd heard it all before, he'd fallen himself, and he was glad to welcome me to what theologian Howard Thurman called "the human frailty."[12]

Today, when people share their brokenness with me, my first goal is to create safe space where they can give voice to whatever they thought was unspeakable—and learn, in the words of theologian Paul Tillich, to "accept the fact that they are accepted."[13] My ultimate goal is to be able to say, from the depths of my own human experience, "Welcome to the human race."

Those words save us from the terrible sense of isolation that comes when we are visited by the "crowd of sorrows" that Rumi writes about in "The Guest House." Those words help us stay faithful to the task of becoming fully human in a world where we can neither survive nor thrive until we embrace the human frailty with reverence and respect.

Confessing My Complicity

In the midst of yet another outbreak of white violence aimed at people of color, my friend Jerry Colonna, chair of the board at Naropa University, tweeted a lovingkindness, or—as Buddhists call it—*mettā* meditation about his struggle with the state of American politics. Yes, even the good guys tweet.

He began, "With apologies to Saint Francis . . . Lord grant me the serenity not to bite the hook of my anger and fear." When I read that line I thought, "Jerry has looked right into my soul and got me dead to rights." In my religious tradition, when you've seen your own failings, there's only one way forward: confess, ask forgiveness, forgive yourself, and try to get it right next time.

My confession is simple. Daily, I get hooked on my anger about our arrogant and unprincipled president, the poisonous aquifer of white nationalism into which he has deliberately tapped, and the endless assaults on almost everything I hold to be good, true, and beautiful. I also get hooked on my fear, but it's not about "those people" our forty-fifth president wants us to fear. I fear this president and the harm he's done to my brothers and sisters in the United States and abroad, to American democracy, to world peace, and to the earth itself.

Jerry doesn't say that there's anything wrong with anger, and I'm glad for that. If I weren't angry about what's going down in Washington, DC, I'd feel like I'd become dumb and numb, and I refuse to go there. Being dumb (and I include myself here) is what got us into this disgusting and dangerous mess, and going numb will keep us in the mess while it gets worse and worse.

Anger isn't the problem. The problem is getting hooked on anger—addicted to an emotion that gives you a fleeting high but leaves you feeling worse, all the while robbing you of well-being and creating an insatiable desire for the next hit. Being hooked saps me of energy and harms my health. Worse still, it diverts me from taking personal responsibility for what's going on right now. Here, too, Jerry's mettā meditation spoke to my condition:

> Grant me the wisdom to see my own unconscious biases that continue to unintentionally and inadvertently make me complicit in this staggering rise of hate and callousness. May I never forget that hate and callousness have been as much part of this American experiment as joy, hope, and love. That while this experience may be new to my consciousness it has been a part of the lives of my fellow Americans who have lacked the access to money and power that come with privilege.

Some will say that Jerry is calling for a fruitless exercise in self-flagellation. I beg to differ. He's calling us to self-examination and self-awareness. It's a call that goes back at least as far as Socrates, who believed that the unexamined life is not worth living. To which I'd add, the unexamined life is a threat to others.

So, for the umpteenth time, I'm trying to come to terms with my own complicity in white privilege and the injustice and inhumanity that flow from it. When white people like me ignore or deny all that, it's just another way of aiding and abetting it.

Isn't the evidence clear-cut? A lot of things that are easy and safe for white folks are difficult or dangerous for people of color—from being pulled over for a broken taillight to trying to rent or buy a home in certain neighborhoods. Being president while black is obviously more perilous than it is while white. If Barack Obama had said any of the most egregious things our forty-fifth president has said, or had had any similar business- or family-related "irregularities," his political career would have flamed out in disgrace. White privilege is powerful. It becomes even more so when we refuse to acknowledge its reality in ourselves and in our culture.

But my confession needs to go deeper than acknowledging my own white privilege. Like many people of my race, I harbor unconscious elements of white supremacy. If I want to stand against the bloody tide that rises on this toxic belief, I must become fully conscious of that fact.

No, I don't belong to or support the KKK and its kin, whose beliefs and actions are evil to the core. But it's a cop-out to limit white supremacy to its most noxious forms. Doing so takes the onus off people like me to come to terms with reality—our country's and our own. How could a nation built in part on the enslavement of black human beings not have a cultural substrate of white supremacy? How could white people rooted in that ground not be tainted by that toxicity?

When I look at myself closely and honestly, I see a form of white supremacy that's subtle but pernicious. For a long time I held an unacknowledged assumption that "white is normal," that white ways are the "normal" ways. All other ways are "exotic" at best, often "strange" and even "off-putting," and sometimes "scary."

I suppose all subcultures believe their ways are normal. But in a nation grounded in the enslavement of black people, only white people get support for that illusion. We don't need a "white history month" to celebrate our contributions to civilization. We don't need to encourage each other to believe that "white is beautiful." We don't need to proclaim "white lives matter." In America, where white people have ruled supreme from day one, all of that comes our way free of charge.

On a planet where white people are in the minority, the arrogance of "white is normal" is breathtaking—and like all arrogance, it distorts one's view of self and world. For example, for fifty years, I've written and spoken about the dangers of the American tendency to make those who are not white, straight, Christian, etc., into "the other."

But not until the last couple of decades did I understand that I am "the other" to many. I'd reserved that category for people who didn't fit my delusional "norm." I didn't hate or fear the other, but seeing otherness in everyone except myself and "my people" is the road to a sense of superiority and even uglier destinations.

Does all of this make me guilty of something sinister simply because I was born white? Of course not. No one is born guilty of anything. The guilt comes when I deny that my whiteness gives me social advantages and makes my view of the world distorted and dishonest. Denial keeps me from owning my own arrogance, putting on corrective lenses, and fully joining the fight against the pestilence of white supremacy.

Is there any hope for white illusionists like me? As far as I'm concerned, this entire essay is about hope, a virtue that takes root in us as soon as we gain self-awareness, confess our role in creating injustice, and reach deep for ways to release the better angels of our nature.

My friend Valarie Kaur is a civil rights activist—a lawyer, a filmmaker, and Sikh justice leader—whose community has suffered xenophobic violence. She has been helping me understand what hope in action looks like through her Revolutionary Love Project, which envisions a world where love is a public ethic and shared practice.[14]

In a recent newsletter, Valarie wrote, "White supremacy is as old as America. But so are acts of Revolutionary Love—and every act of love inspires another." Then she spoke to the skeptics:

> If you cringe when people say love is the answer, I do too—I'm a lawyer. In America, we only talk about love as a feeling that happens to us if we're lucky. If love is just a good feeling, then of course it is too fickle, too sentimental, too fleeting to be a force in the face of injustice.

Through a feminist, woman-of-color lens—inspired by the Sikh concept of the warrior-saint—Valarie is redefining and reviving the great tradition of nonviolent action in terms that respond to what Martin Luther King Jr. called "the fierce urgency of now."[15]

Revolutionary Love is not romantic but embodied, courageous, and demanding. When I asked her to describe it for me, Valarie drew on her experience of becoming a mother—from the labor pains that can feel like dying, to a lifetime of being gentle and fierce in nurturing and protecting the child you love:

> Mothering—a capacity that exists within all of us—helps us redefine love, not just as emotion but as a form of sweet labor. It calls us to "see no stranger," to tend to their wounds *and* our own, and to breathe and push through all the emotions that come with that labor: Joy is the gift of love. Grief is the price of love. Anger is the force that protects that which is loved.
>
> Choosing to practice the love ethic can birth new possibilities. But to be revolutionary, love must be poured in three directions: toward others, toward our opponents, and toward ourselves. Revolutionary Love is the call of our times.

When I find myself once again "biting the hook of anger" instead of using my anger to protect my capacity to love, and have the guts to ask myself why, I have only one honest answer. Being hooked drains me of morale, energy, and courage, sparing me from the challenges of practicing Revolutionary Love.

Awakened by Jerry Colonna and animated by Valarie Kaur, I'm practicing a daily two-part gut-check:

1. Where am I today with my "white is normal" delusion?
2. Am I willing to risk practicing the warrior-saint love that, as Valarie says, "has the power to transform our interior life, our relationships, and social conditions"?

When confession opens the door to hope, and we go through, the next step is action. If you wonder what Revolutionary Love in action looks like, I urge you to sign the Declaration of Revolutionary Love.[16] It will connect you to the movement and its resources—including Valarie Kaur's TED Talk and forthcoming book, educational curricula, conferences, stories on film and TV, action plans of various sorts, and emerging opportunities for training and action in this next-generation embodiment of revolutionary nonviolence.

The world needs this revolution. America needs it. People of color need it. And white people like me need it, perhaps most of all, if we want to live in service of the twined causes of love, truth, and justice.

Heartbreak and Hope for New Life

A disciple asks the rebbe: "Why does Torah tell us to 'place these words upon your hearts'? Why does it not tell us to place these holy words in our hearts?" The rebbe answers: "It is because as we are, our hearts are closed, and we cannot place the holy words in our hearts. So we place them on top of our hearts. And there they stay until, one day, the heart breaks and the words fall in."

—HASIDIC TALE[17]

Heartbreak comes with the territory called being human. When love and trust fail us, when what once brought meaning goes dry, when a dream drifts out of reach, when a devastating disease strikes, or when someone precious to us dies, our hearts break and we suffer.

What can we do with our pain? How might we hold it and work with it? How do we turn the power of suffering toward new life? The way we answer those questions is critical because *violence is what happens when we don't know what else to do with our suffering.*

Violence is not limited to inflicting physical harm. We do violence every time we violate the sanctity of the human self, our own or another person's. Sometimes we try to numb the pain of suffering in ways that dishonor our souls. We turn to noise, frenzy, nonstop work, and substance abuse as anesthetics that only deepen our suffering. Sometimes we visit violence upon others, as if causing them pain would mitigate our own. Racism, sexism, homophobia, and contempt for the poor are among the cruel outcomes of this demented strategy.

Nations, too, answer suffering with violence. On September 11, 2001, three thousand Americans died from acts of terrorism. America needed to respond, so plans for war were laid. Few were troubled by the fact that the country we eventually attacked had little or nothing to do with the terrorists who attacked us. We had suffered; we needed to do violence to someone, somewhere; and so we went to war, at tragic cost. The best estimates of the total war casualties in Iraq since the US-led invasion range from 500,000 to 1,000,000 souls.[18] Forty-five hundred Americans died in Iraq, and so many came home with grave wounds to body and mind that thousands more have been fatalities of war via suicide.[19]

When we lack the moral imagination to do something else with our suffering, we do violence. But it's possible to ride the power of suffering toward new life—it happens every day. We all know people who've suffered the loss of the most important person in their lives. At first, they disappear into grief, certain that life will never again be worth living. But, through the passage of time and various forms of inner work, they slowly emerge to find that their hearts have grown larger and more compassionate. They have developed a greater capacity to take in others' sorrows and joys—not in spite of their loss but because of it.

Suffering breaks our hearts, but the heart can break in two quite different ways. There's the brittle heart that breaks into shards, shattering the one who suffers as it explodes, and sometimes taking others down when it's thrown like a grenade at the ostensible source of its pain.

Then there's the supple heart, the one that breaks open, not apart, the one that can grow into greater capacity for the many forms of love. Only the supple heart can hold suffering in a way that opens to new life.

How can I make my heart more supple? The answer, I think, is to exercise my heart by stretching it, the way a runner stretches the leg muscles to avoid injury. With regular exercise, my heart is less likely to break apart into shards that may become shrapnel, and more likely to break open into largeness. These days, my opportunities for heart-stretching increase along with the losses that come with aging, and it all comes down to this: take it in, take it all in.

My heart is stretched every time I'm able to take in life's little deaths without an anesthetic: a friendship gone sour, a mean-spirited critique of my work, failure at a task that was important to me. I can also exercise my heart by taking in life's little joys: a small kindness from a stranger, the sound of a distant train reviving childhood memories, the infectious giggle of a two-year-old as I "hide" and then "leap out" from behind cupped hands. Taking all of it in—the good and the bad alike—is a form of exercise that slowly transforms my clenched fist of a heart into an open hand.

Does a nation-state have a heart that can become supple enough to respond to collective suffering without violence? I doubt it. But since I don't know for sure—and never will if I don't keep the question alive—I'm not going to yield to cynicism. There are enough real-world facts and possibilities to justify hope.[20]

Remember how people around the world stood in unity with us for a few weeks after September 11, 2001? "Today," they said, "we, too, are Americans," because they had known suffering at least as painful as ours. Suppose we'd been able to take in the global flood of compassion that came our way during those post-9/11 days. We might have been given the grace to consider the alternative to war many proposed at the time, including the late theologian and activist, William Sloane Coffin:

We will respond, but not in kind. We will not seek to avenge the death of innocent Americans by the death of innocent victims elsewhere, lest we become what we abhor. We refuse to ratchet up the cycle of violence that brings only ever more death, destruction and deprivation. What we will do is build coalitions with other nations. We will share intelligence, freeze assets, and engage in forceful extradition of terrorists if internationally sanctioned. [We will] do all in [our] power to see justice done, but by the force of law only, never the law of force.[21]

That proposal was aimed at turning suffering toward new life. Sadly, as a nation, we lacked the moral imagination and capacity of heart to respond to our suffering with anything other than massive violence. So today we are living into Coffin's prophecy of "ever more death, destruction and deprivation." We have traveled some distance, I fear, toward becoming "what we abhor."

Alternative responses to suffering are within reach in our personal and political lives. Will we use them? It depends on our willingness to exercise our hearts—individually and collectively—so that when suffering strikes, they will break open to new life.

That's why Mary Oliver gave us this heart-wrenching poem—whose title refers to the heavy metal that pollutes our waterways and kills wildlife—a poem to exercise our hearts:

Lead

Here is a story
to break your heart.
Are you willing?
This winter
the loons came to our harbor
and died, one by one,
of nothing we could see.
A friend told me
of one on the shore
that lifted its head and opened
the elegant beak and cried out
in the long, sweet savoring of its life
which, if you have heard it,
you know is a sacred thing,
and for which, if you have not heard it,
you had better hurry to where
they still sing.
And, believe me, tell no one
just where that is.
The next morning
this loon, speckled
and iridescent and with a plan
to fly home
to some hidden lake,
was dead on the shore.
I tell you this
to break your heart,
by which I mean only
that it break open and never close again
to the rest of the world.[22]

A Season of Paradox

Autumn

The leaves are falling, falling as if from far up,
as if orchards were dying high in space.
Each leaf falls as if it were motioning "no."

And tonight the heavy earth is falling
away from all other stars in the loneliness.

We're all falling. This hand here is falling.
And look at the other one. It's in them all.

And yet there is Someone, whose hands
infinitely calm, holding up all this falling.

—Rainer Maria Rilke[23]

Autumn in my part of the world is a season of bounty and beauty. It's also a season of steady decline—and, for some of us, a slow slide into melancholy. The days become shorter and colder, the trees shed their glory, and summer's abundance starts to decay toward winter's death.

I'm a professional melancholic, and for years my delight in the autumn color show quickly morphed into sadness as I watched the beauty die. Focused on the browning of summer's green growth, I allowed the prospect of death to eclipse all that's life-giving about fall and its sensuous delights.

Then I began to understand a simple fact: all the "falling" that's going on out there is full of promise. Seeds are being planted and leaves are being composted as earth prepares for yet another uprising of green.

Today, as I weather the late autumn of my own life, I find nature a trustworthy guide. It's easy to fixate on everything that goes to ground as time goes by: the disintegration of a relationship, the disappearance of good work well done, the diminishment of a sense of purpose and meaning. But as I've come to understand that life "composts" and "seeds" *us* as autumn does the earth, I've seen how possibility gets planted in us even in the hardest of times.

Looking back, I see how the job I lost pushed me to find work that was mine to do, how the "Road Closed" sign turned me toward terrain I'm glad I traveled, how losses that felt irredeemable forced me to find new sources of meaning. In each of these experiences, it felt as though something was dying, and so it was. Yet deep down, amid all the falling, the seeds of new life were always being silently and lavishly sown.

The hopeful notion that new life is hidden in dying is surely reinforced by the visual glories of autumn. What artist would paint a deathbed scene with the vibrant and vital palette nature uses? Perhaps death possesses a grace that we who fear dying, who find it ugly and even obscene, cannot see. How shall we understand nature's testimony that dying itself—as devastating as we know it can be—contains the hope of a certain beauty?

The closest I've ever come to answering that question begins with these words from Thomas Merton, quoted earlier in this book: "There is in all visible things . . . a hidden wholeness."[24]

In the visible world of nature, a great truth is concealed in plain sight. Diminishment and beauty, darkness and light, death and life are not opposites: they are held together in the paradox of the "hidden wholeness." In a paradox, opposites do not negate each other—they cohabit and cocreate in mysterious unity at the heart of reality. Deeper still, they need each other for health, just as our well-being depends on breathing in and breathing out.

Because we live in a culture that prefers the ease of either-or to the complexities of both-and, we have a hard time holding opposites together. We want light without darkness, the glories of spring and summer without the demands of autumn and winter, the pleasures of life without the pangs of death. We make Faustian bargains hoping to get what we want, but they never truly enliven us and cannot possibly sustain us in hard times.

When we so fear the dark that we demand light around the clock, there can be only one result: artificial light that is glaring and graceless and, beyond its borders, a darkness that grows ever more terrifying as we try to hold it off. Split off from each other, neither darkness nor light is fit for human habitation. But the moment we say "Yes" to both of them and join their paradoxical dance, the two conspire to make us healthy and whole.

When I give myself over to organic reality—to the endless interplay of darkness and light, falling and rising—the life I am given is as real and colorful, fruitful and whole as this graced and graceful world and the seasonal cycles that make it so. Though I still grieve as beauty goes to ground, autumn reminds me to celebrate the primal power that is forever making all things new in me, in us, and in the natural world.

Appalachian Autumn

No, I'm not as old as the hills
that rise around me as I rest
amid the tawny grasses of this
holler. But here in late October
of my seventy-third year, they
feel like age-mates to me. The
greens of spring and summer
are long-gone from the trees.
Leaves of crimson, burnt
umber and amber flare against
the darkening sky, defying
with beauty the soon-to-end
cycle of one more round of
life and love in this longtime landscape of suffering.

The ancient earth takes it all in,
indifferent and compassionate
in the same breath. This is how
I want to live, my failings and
lost opportunities forgiven
as they are under this sun—
released in their triviality,
resurrected as new life—
en route to dying with
thanks and praise and no
mind-begotten regrets.

—PARKER J. PALMER

VII. Over the Edge

Where We Go When We Die

Introduction

At some point in my forties, I was introduced to the Rule of Saint Benedict, a spiritual classic, "written by Benedict of Nursia (c. AD 480–550) for monks living communally under the authority of an abbot [or abbess]."[1] The Rule became the basis for the Order of Saint Benedict, a community very much alive today around the world.[2]

One of Benedict's precepts instructs the monks to "keep death daily before one's eyes."[3] The first time I read that line, it struck me as a bummer. Why should I look away from my vital and engaged life to contemplate my mortality? Now that some years have passed, I know at least two good answers to that question.

One comes from Brother David Steindl-Rast, himself a Benedictine monk:

> The finality of death is meant to challenge us to decision, the decision to be fully present here now, and so begin eternal life. For eternity rightly understood is

not the perpetuation of time, on and on, but rather the overcoming of time by the now that does not pass away.[4]

Brother David's version of "eternal life" is one I can embrace, now that I understand the rewards of being "fully present here now." No need to wait until you die to collect your rewards in some heaven on high. Pay attention to what's right here, right now, and you'll be rewarded immediately—the Beloved Community is in our midst. Rightly understood, keeping death "daily before one's eyes" does not mean looking away from one's life. It means looking more deeply into it.

The second reason I need to keep death daily before my eyes is also rooted in my experience. Nothing makes me more grateful for life—even in the hard times—than remembering that it's a pure gift that I didn't earn and won't have forever. Nothing motivates me more strongly to "pay it forward" than knowing that the time to share a gift is when I have it in hand.

The subtitle of this chapter is "Where We Go When We Die." Please forgive the lack of truth in advertising, but my information on this topic is quite limited. If there's been a definitive statement on the matter, I didn't get the memo. So there are only two essays here, plus a poem.

The first essay, "Fierce with Reality," springs from my conviction that the most important thing we can do to prepare for death is to show up as our true selves as often as we can while we have life. As Brother David says, it's vital to be fully present in the moment, and to be present with all we have, aware of our shadow as well as our light.

"A Wilderness Pilgrimage" is about an annual visit my wife and I make to the Boundary Waters Canoe Area (BWCA) of northern Minnesota. The BWCA is one of my "thin places," as Celtic Christians called them—a place where "the veil between worlds" is more transparent and one can catch a glimpse of whatever lies beyond it. I don't know exactly where we go when we die, but the BWCA (aka God's Country) strikes me as an ultimate tourist destination.

"Waving Goodbye from Afar" is a poem I wrote on a day when the deaths of four longtime friends in the course of a single year hit me with special poignancy. I felt sad that I was unable to be with any of them when they died. But as the poem unfolded, I began to understand how my absence might have made that journey easier for my friends, and might be seen as a final gift from me.

Fierce with Reality

Early in this book, I quoted psychologist Florida Scott-Maxwell. I want to quote her again as I move toward the end: "You need only claim the events of your life to make yourself yours. When you truly possess all you have been and done . . . you are fierce with reality."[5]

Scott-Maxwell was eighty-five when she wrote those words. I first read them when I was half her age, but I knew she was speaking directly to me. At age forty-three,

I was succeeding and failing as a husband and a father on a daily basis; had done battle with racism as a community organizer while remaining oblivious to the fortress of white privilege that protected me from its evils; was alternately laid low and energized by the rejections I received en route to becoming a writer; and had nearly drowned and then surfaced from my first descent into clinical depression.

I was, in short, a reasonably normal person, a complex and conflicted soul who yearned to be whole. I wanted a life of personal fulfillment that served the world well—a life of love for self and others—and I knew that getting there would require me to be "fierce with reality." But I devoutly wished for an easier path than the one Scott-Maxwell recommends. At age forty-three, I didn't have the courage required to "truly possess all [I had] been and done."

Today, as I close in on eighty, I know there are no shortcuts to wholeness. The only way to become whole is to put our arms lovingly around *everything* we know ourselves to be: self-serving and generous, spiteful and compassionate, cowardly and courageous, treacherous and trustworthy. We must be able to say to ourselves and to the world at large, "I am *all* of the above." If we can't embrace the whole of who we are—embrace it with transformative love—we'll imprison the creative energies hidden in our own shadows and be unable to engage creatively with the world's complex mix of shadow and light.

Of course, naming, claiming, and loving the whole of who we are is easier said than done: honest self-examination is a well-known source of human misery. But the alternative is more painful still. Psychologist Erik Erikson, in his scheme of adult development, argues that if we can't accept all that we've been and done, we'll age away from "integrity" toward "despair."[6]

As I look around at my age-mates, it's easy to find cases of the latter and see its sad consequences. Some consequences are personal, as when people who try to deny their inner darkness carry and spread it around wherever they go. Some consequences are political, as when people who fear whatever feels alien in themselves project their fear on the "alien other"—while shameless politicians cynically manipulate that fear as they play the dangerous divide-and-conquer game.

But if we are willing to move through the gravitas of honest self-examination toward the grace of compassionate self-acceptance, the rewards are great. When we can say, "I am *all* of the above, my shadow as well as my light," we become more at ease in our own skins, more at home on the face of a planet rich with diversity, more accepting of others who are no more or less broken-whole than we are, and better able to live as life-givers to the end of our days.

How can we learn to embrace with love the whole of who we are—a task that need not and should not await our elder years? Of course there are tried-and-true aids such as meditation, journaling, and therapy, all of which have been helpful to me. Here are three others that I sometimes find even more helpful:

1. Reach out to the younger generation—not to advise them but to learn from them, gain energy from them, and support them on their way. Erik Erikson called this kind of reaching out "generativity," an alternative to the "stagnation" of age that sooner or later leads to despair.
2. Move *toward* whatever you fear, not away from it. I try to remember the advice I was given on an Outward Bound course when I was frozen with fear on a rock face in the middle of a 100-foot rappel: "If you can't get out of it, get into it!" If, for example, you fear "the other," get into his or her story face-to-face, and watch your fear shrink as your empathy expands.
3. Spend time in the natural world, as much time as you can. Nature constantly reminds me that everything has a place, that nothing need be excluded. That "mess" on the forest floor—like the messes in my own life—has an amazing integrity and harmony to it.

Once more with feeling, my mantra: *Wholeness is the goal, but wholeness does not mean perfection. It means embracing brokenness as an integral part of life.* The sooner we understand this, the better. It's a truth that can set us free to live well, to love well, and, in the end, to die well.

I can't think of a sadder way to die than with the knowledge that I never showed up in this world as who I really am. I can't think of a more graced way to die than with the knowledge that I showed up here as my true self, as best I knew how, able to engage life freely and lovingly because I had become fierce with reality.

A Wilderness Pilgrimage

Their Slow Way

Let these woods have their
slow way with you. Patient
pines that hold their green
through all the frozen seasons,
lichen-covered rocks that live
indifferent to time's passage—
these will teach you how to
bring your life to ground.

The fractal chaos of the forest
floor, its white anemones,
spiked grasses and dead leaves,
the fallen trunks and branches
splayed out like pick-up sticks—
these will teach you how
to live freely, with abandon,
and feed the roots of new growth
when your time has come.

—Parker J. Palmer

Every August for the past twenty years, my wife and I
have visited the Boundary Waters Canoe Area of northern
Minnesota, a million acres of federally protected wilderness
along the Canadian border. Long before I saw this place, a
friend tried to describe it to me. "Everywhere you look," he

said, "there's a perfect Japanese garden." And so there is: rocks, trees, water, and sky in endless permutations of elegance.

I've been on a lake in the BWCA on many flawless August evenings when the heavy, moist heat of the day has given way to cool breezes that stir my mind and heart, even as they stir the water. A low-lying sun bathes the forest in honey. The pines, aspens, weed trees, bushes, and tufted grasses glow amber and green against what e. e. cummings called a "blue true dream of sky."[7]

I was in my late fifties when I first spent time in this patch of heaven. Its simplicity, beauty, and peace fed me so deeply that I've returned every summer since then. At first, vacation was all I had in mind. But I soon realized that my annual trek to the Boundary Waters was a pilgrimage to holy ground, a place of healing.

During the workaday year, when things get tough, I make this pilgrimage in my imagination. I close my eyes and see myself hiking through the sun-dappled woods, paddling down a windswept lake, hearing the unforgettable call of a loon, watching the cosmic drama of the Northern Lights, or eavesdropping on the quiet conversation between those two old friends—the lake and the land—as the cold, clear water laps gently against the shore.

It's not tranquility alone that makes this wilderness a place of healing for me. It's the patient, resourceful, resilient way nature heals itself, showing me what it takes to heal my own wounds so I can be in the world as a wounded healer. Watching wilderness overcome devastation has helped me see how suffering can serve as a seedbed for renewal. Even more, it has offered reassurance that in the great cycle of life and death, new life always gets the last word.

On July 4, 1999, a derecho—a line of fierce, fast-moving windstorms that create an inland hurricane— ripped through the Boundary Waters.[8] It took down millions of trees, creating tinder for numerous fires that were to ravage even more forest over the next few years. A month after the derecho, when I arrived for my annual retreat, the sight of that massive blowdown broke my heart. I wondered if I could stay or would want to return the next year. But something held me there and has kept me coming back, giving me a chance to witness resurrection.

Prior to the blowdown, one of my favorite hikes passed through a section of forest so thick it felt primeval. Knowing that this cloistered woods had been hard-hit by wind, then fire, it was several years before I felt able to try that trail again. When I did, I saw how the void created by death had been filling with new life.

Raspberries and blueberries, lupine and purple asters had sprung up in abundance as sunlight fell on earth that had long been shrouded in shadow. Aspens grew from seedlings at the speed of a hungry teenager; today, two decades after the derecho, most of those seedlings are twice my height. And the massive rocks this trail traverses now look like raku pottery, fired in the kiln of a fierce-burning forest, glazed in metallic shimmers of red and brown, blue and gold.

For years, I've asked myself the ancient question, "How, then, shall we live?" I've often found good guidance on the time-honored paths of the world's great wisdom traditions. But at age seventy-nine, as I also ask "How, then, shall we die?" no path serves me better than those I've tracked through the Boundary Waters. It's a place where, time and again, I'm taken to "the brink of everything" and given a glimpse into heaven.

Theologies that portray heaven as a gated community in the sky don't speak to my condition. Among other things, an eternity spent exclusively among members of my own tribe sounds more hellish than heavenly. Nor am I persuaded by claims that, when we die, spirit separates from matter and takes on some sort of disembodied, wraithlike life. As far as I can tell, matter and spirit are intertwined and indivisible, a distinction without a difference, two sides of one coin. If flesh and earth were not infused with spirit, how could we and the natural world be so full of beauty, healing, and grace?

I learned long ago how much I do not know, so I won't be shocked if death has surprises in store for me. But amid all my not-knowing, I'm certain of two things: when we die, our bodies return to the earth, and earth knows how to turn death into new life. When my own small life ends in some version of wind and fire, my body will be transformed by the same alchemy that keeps making all things new, witness this wilderness. As the medieval alchemists dreamed, dross will be turned into gold.

It matters not to me whether I am resurrected in a loon calling from the lake, a sun-glazed pine, a wildflower on the forest floor, the stuff that fertilizes those trees and flowers, or the Northern Lights and the stars that lie beyond them. It's all good and it's all gold, a vast web of life in which body and spirit are one.

I won't be glad to say goodbye to life, to challenges that help me grow, to gifts freely given, or to everyone and everything I love. But I'll be glad to play a bit part in making new life possible for others. That's a prospect that makes life worth dying for.

Twenty annual pilgrimages to this holy place called the Boundary Waters have convinced me that Julian of Norwich got it right: "All shall be well, and all shall be well, and all manner of thing shall be well."[9]

Waving Goodbye from Afar
(for Angie, Ian, Vincent, and John)

One by one, their names have been
exhaled in recent weeks, fading into thin air
on their final breath: Angie. Ian. Vincent. John.

I talked, laughed and worked with them, we
cared about each other. Now they are gone.
No, they do not live on—just watch the world

keep turning in their absence, a tribute here
and there depending on the fame of the fast-
fading name. I've always thought it would

be good if a few who loved me sat with me
as I died. Now, as I learn of friends who've
taken sudden leave, I'm glad all I can do is

wave goodbye from afar, knowing they can't
see me. It feels right to offer them an unseen
final salute, seeking no attention, unable to

distract them from a journey each of us must
make alone. It must be a breathless climb, the
kind I've made many times in the mountains

of New Mexico. The last thing I wanted there
was someone who just had to talk, when it was
all I could do to climb, to breathe, then stop—

marveling at the view, wondering what's up top.
—PARKER J. PALMER

Postlude

Why Should I Ever Be Sad

Why should I ever be sad,
knowing the aspens are
always here dancing along
this trail, slim as willowy
girls, swinging their arms,
tossing their hair, swaying
their hips in rhythm with
the mountain wind. Above
the aspens, intensified sky,
a dream of blue seen only as
cities fade from view. Below
them a rocky slope covered
with clotted clumps of leaves
and fallen, rotted branches,
laying down a love bed where
Indian Paintbrush and white
violets grow amid a flourish
of green. All of the tumbled
boulders and rocks have found
their angle of perfect repose,

so why should I ever be sad?
All of this waits for me when
at last I stumble and fall,
waits for me to join in this
dance with all that turns and
whirls—a dance done to the
silent music of our dappled,
singing, swaying world.

—Parker J. Palmer

Two Toasts

To Words and How They Live Between Us . . .
Praise be that this thin mark, this sound
Can form the word that takes on flesh
To enter where no flesh can go
To fill each other's emptiness.

To Us and How We Live Between the Words . . .
And in between the sound of words
I hear your silent, sounding soul
Where One abides in solitude
Who keeps us one when speech shall go.

—Parker J. Palmer

The song "Two Toasts" (music by Carrie Newcomer and words by Parker J. Palmer) can be downloaded free of charge at NewcomerPalmer.com /home.

Notes

Prelude

1. Kurt Vonnegut, *Player Piano* (New York: Dell Publishing, 1980), 84.
2. Leonard Cohen, "A Thousand Kisses Deep," *The Leonard Cohen Files,* http://tinyurl.com/y9bkha66.
3. Dylan Thomas, "Do not go gentle into that good night," in *The Poems of Dylan Thomas* (New York: New Directions, 1971).
4. William James, *The Varieties of Religious Experience* (New York: Cosimo Classics, 2007), 18.
5. These words were famously spoken by Truman Capote to put down other writers' work. See Quote Investigator, http://tinyurl.com/y8grfr55.
6. *Online Etymology Dictionary,* s.v. "Levity" (accessed January 13, 2018), http://tinyurl.com/ybbbyjrv.
7. G. K. Chesterton, *Orthodoxy* (New York: Simon & Brown, 2016), 95.
8. Leonard Cohen, "Tower of Song," *The Leonard Cohen Files,* http://tinyurl.com/yaosaqzr.
9. "Invocation" from *Shaking the Tree* by Jeanne Lohmann. Reprinted with permission from Fithian Press, a division of Daniel & Daniel Publishers, Inc.

10. Some of these essays first appeared on the On Being Studios blog. A list of my *On Being* posts from October 5, 2014, onward is at http://tinyurl.com/ybwmhkbe.

I. The View from the Brink: What I Can See from Here

1. *Cambridge Dictionary,* s.v. "Brink" (accessed January 13, 2018), http://tinyurl.com/y8npy22z.
2. Oliver Wendell Holmes, *Holmes-Pollock Letters: The Correspondence of Mr. Justice Holmes and Sir Frederick Pollock, 1874–1932,* 2nd ed. (Belknap Press, 1961), 109.
3. Courtney E. Martin, "Reuniting with Awe," *On Being* (blog), March 6, 2015, http://tinyurl.com/ybdjhwa9.
4. Florida Scott-Maxwell, *The Measure of My Days* (New York: Penguin Books, 1983), 42.
5. *Wikipedia, The Free Encyclopedia,* s.v. "Thomas Aquinas" (accessed January 11, 2018), http://tinyurl.com/npo9d4u.
6. "The World: Love" from *Czesław Milosz New and Collected Poems: 1931–2001.* Copyright © 1988, 1991, 1995, 2001 by Czesław Milosz Royalties, Inc. Reprinted with permission from HarperCollins Publishers, and Penguin Random House Ltd.
7. William Butler Yeats, "The Coming of Wisdom with Time," Bartleby.com, http://tinyurl.com/hu9thkt
8. Emily Dickinson, "Tell the truth but tell it slant—(1263)," Poetry Foundation, http://tinyurl.com/hh2cm5w.
9. Saul McLeod, "Erik Erikson," *Simply Psychology* (2017), http://tinyurl.com/7svu5fu.
10. Lucille Clifton, "the death of fred clifton" from *Collected Poems of Lucille Clifton: 1965–2010.* Copyright © 1987, 1989 by Lucille Clifton. Published by BOA Editions. Reprinted with permission of The Permissions Company, Inc., on behalf of BOA Editions, Ltd., www.boaeditions.org, and Curtis Brown, Ltd.

II. Young and Old: The Dance of the Generations

1. Oliver Wendell Holmes, "The Voiceless," in *The Complete Poetical Works of Oliver Wendell Holmes* (New York: Houghton, Mifflin, 1900), 99.
2. Nelle Morton, *The Journey Is Home* (Boston: Beacon Press, 1985), 55. See also "Nelle Katherine Morton Facts," *Your Dictionary,* http://biography.yourdictionary.com/nelle-katherine-morton.
3. Howard Thurman, *The Inward Journey* (Richmond, IN: Friends United Press, 2007), 77.
4. Courtney Martin, *Do It Anyway: The New Generation of Activists* (Boston: Beacon Press, 2013).
5. Parker J. Palmer, *The Courage to Teach: Exploring the Inner Landscape of a Teacher's Life, 20th anniversary ed.* (San Francisco: Jossey-Bass, 2017), 26.
6. Mohandas K. Gandhi, *Gandhi: An Autobiography—The Story of My Experiments with Truth* (Boston: Beacon Press, 1993).
7. Rainer Maria Rilke, *Letters to a Young Poet,* trans. Joan M. Burnham (New York: New World Library, 2000), 35.
8. Terrence Real, *I Don't Want to Talk About It: Overcoming the Secret Legacy of Male Depression* (New York: Scribner, 1998).
9. "The simplicity on the other side of complexity" quoted in John Paul Lederach, *The Moral Imagination: The Art and Soul of Building Peace* (Oxford, UK: Oxford University Press, 2010), 31.
10. Diane Ackerman, *A Natural History of the Senses* (New York: Vintage Books, 1991), 309.

III. Getting Real: From Illusion to Reality

1. *Crossings Reflection #4: "The Sound of the Genuine," Rev. Dr. Howard Thurman, (1899–1981)* (Indianapolis: University

of Indianapolis: The Crossings Project, n.d.), http://tlnyuil .com/gmv2ux2. For more on the Crossings Project and its publications, see http://tinyurl.com/zbmyaqf.

2. Thomas Merton, *The Asian Journal of Thomas Merton* (New York: New Directions, 1975), 307.

3. Thomas Merton, *The Seven Storey Mountain, 50th Anniversary Edition* (New York: Harcourt Brace, 1998).

4. Herbert Mason, *The Death of al-Hallaj* (Notre Dame, IN: Notre Dame Press, 1979), xix.

5. Thomas Merton, *The Inner Experience: Notes on Contemplation* (San Francisco: HarperSanFrancisco, 2004), 4.

6. Thomas Merton, *The Sign of Jonas* (New York: Harcourt Brace, 1953), 11.

7. These words are attributed to Bohr in many secondary sources, though I've been unable to find them in his published works. Their authenticity is confirmed by a remark made by his son, Hans Bohr, in an essay called "My Father": "One of the favorite maxims of my father was the distinction between the two sorts of truths, profound truths recognized by the fact that the opposite is also a profound truth, in contrast to trivialities where opposites are obviously absurd." In *Niels Bohr: His Life and Work as Seen by His Friends and Colleagues,* ed. Stefan Rozental (Hoboken, NJ: Wiley, 1967), 328.

8. Thomas Merton, "To Each His Darkness," in *Raids on the Unspeakable* (New York: New Directions, 1966), 11–12.

9. Rainer Maria Rilke, *Letters to a Young Poet,* trans. M. D. Herter (New York: Norton, 1993), 59.

10. Parker J. Palmer, *Let Your Life Speak* (San Francisco: Jossey-Bass, 2000), chap. 2.

11. For more information about the Center for Courage & Renewal, see http://www.CourageRenewal.org.

12. Merton, *Asian Journal*, 338.
13. Ibid.
14. Chinua Achebe, *Things Fall Apart* (New York: Anchor Books, 1994).
15. Thomas Merton, "Hagia Sophia," in *A Thomas Merton Reader*, ed. Thomas P. McDonnell (New York: Doubleday, 1989), 506.
16. Thomas Merton, *The Hidden Ground of Love* (New York: Farrar, Straus & Giroux, 1985), 294.
17. Igumen Chariton of Valamo, *The Art of Prayer: An Orthodox Anthology* (New York: Farrar, Straus and Giroux, 1966), 20.
18. "Beliefnet's Inspirational Quotes," Beliefnet, http://tinyurl .com/osgyqke.
19. "The Guest House" by Jalal al-Din Rumi and Coleman Barks (Trans.), from *The Essential Rumi* (New York: HarperOne, 2004). Reprinted with permission from the translator, Coleman Barks.
20. Jonathan Montaldo, ed., *A Year with Thomas Merton: Daily Meditations from His Journals* (New York: HarperOne, 2004), 12.
21. Albert Camus, *Lyrical and Critical Essays* (New York: Vintage, 1970), 169.
22. Chuang Tzu, "The Empty Boat," in *The Way of Chuang Tzu*, ed. Thomas Merton (New York: New Directions, 2010), 114.
23. Parker J. Palmer, *A Hidden Wholeness* (San Francisco: Jossey-Bass, 2004), 55.
24. Montaldo, *Year with Thomas Merton*, 14.
25. William James, quoted in Joseph Demakis, *The Ultimate Book of Quotations*, http://tinyurl.com/y9963758.
26. Thomas Merton, *The Sign of Jonas* (New York: Harcourt, Brace and Company, 1953), 37.

27. Aubrey Menen, *The Ramayana, as told by Aubrey Menen* (Westport, CT: Greenwood Press, 1972), 276.

28. Montaldo, *Year with Thomas Merton,* 16.

29. In Richard Kehl, *Silver Departures* (New York: Aladdin, 1991), 8.

30. Montaldo, *Year with Thomas Merton,* 13.

31. Dylan Thomas, "Do not go gentle into that good night," in *The Poems of Dylan Thomas* (New York: New Directions, 1971).

IV. Work and Vocation: Writing a Life

1. Mary Catherine Bateson, *Composing a Life* (New York: Grove Press, 2001).

2. Quote Investigator, http://tinyurl.com/yd5rl8k9.

3. George Orwell, *Why I Write* (New York: Penguin Books, 2005), 10.

4. To learn about the disputed origins of this quip, see Quote Investigator, http://tinyurl.com/y7db9qve.

5. *Wikipedia, The Free Encyclopedia,* s.v. "John Gillespie Magee Jr.: *High Flight,*" (accessed January 11, 2018), http://tinyurl.com/yc9fhbc3.

6. Barry Lopez, *Crossing Open Ground* (New York: Vintage, 1989), 69.

7. Wikiquotes, http://tinyurl.com/yayymvwe.

8. Thomas Merton, *The Inner Experience: Notes on Contemplation* (San Francisco: HarperSanFrancisco, 2004), 4.

9. Thomas Mann, *Essays of Three Decades* (New York: Knopf, 1942).

10. José Ortega y Gasset, *On Love: Aspects of a Single Theme* (Cleveland, OH: World-Meridian, 1957), 121.

11. Bateson, *Composing a Life.*

12. William Wordsworth, "Intimations of Immortality from Recollections of Early Childhood," *The Oxford Book of English Verse, 1250–1918,* ed. Arthur Quiller-Couch (Oxford, UK: Oxford University Press, 1963), 612.

13. Henry David Thoreau, *A Week on the Concord and Merrimack Rivers* (New York: Dover, 2001), 223.

14. Paul Engle, "Poetry Is Ordinary Language Raised to the Nth Power," *New York Times,* February 17, 1957, 4.

15. Robert Penn Warren, "Poetry Is a Kind of Unconscious Autobiography," *New York Times Book Review,* May 12, 1985, 9–10.

16. "To Hayden Carruth" from *Wendell Berry, New Collected Poems.* Copyright © 2012 by Wendell Berry. Reprinted by permission of Counterpoint Press.

17. Shunryu Suzuki, *Zen Mind, Beginner's Mind: Informal Talks on Zen Meditation and Practice* (Boulder, CO: Shambhala, 2011), 1.

V. Keep Reaching Out: Staying Engaged with the World

1. "Santos: New Mexico." Copyright 1948, 1974 by May Sarton, from *Collected Poems 1930–1993* by May Sarton. Used by permission of W. W. Norton & Company, Inc., and Russell & Volkening as agents for the author.

2. Will Oremus, "The Media Have Finally Figured Out How to Cover Trump's Lies," *Slate,* March 23, 2017, http://tinyurl.com/moj2tb4.

3. Anne Lamott, *Traveling Mercies: Some Thoughts on Faith* (New York: Anchor Books, 2000), 134.

4. Iris DeMent, "God May Forgive You (But I Won't)," YouTube, http://tinyurl.com/yaqhfngs.

5. Sarton, "Santos: New Mexico."

6. Parker J. Palmer, *Healing the Heart of Democracy: The Courage to Create a Politics Worthy of the Human Spirit* (San Francisco: Jossey-Bass, 2014). Discussion resources and videos related to the book are available at http://tinyurl.com/hl4zhy9.

7. William Sloane Coffin, *Credo* (Louisville, KY: Westminster John Knox Press, 2004), 84.

8. "How Journalists Are Rethinking Their Role Under a Trump Presidency," *Diane Rhem Show* transcript, November 30, 2016, http://tinyurl.com/hdykgaq.

9. Margaret Sullivan, "The Post-Truth World of the Trump Administration Is Scarier Than You Think," *Washington Post,* December 4, 2016, http://tinyurl.com/zebmkrn.

10. Louis Nelson, "Conway: Judge Trump by What's in His Heart, Not What Comes out of His Mouth," *Politico,* January 9, 2017, http://tinyurl.com/h86donc.

11. D'Angelo Gore, Lori Robertson, and Robert Farley, "Fact-Checking Trump's Press Conference," FactCheck.org, January 11, 2017, http://tinyurl.com/z48vhdc.

12. US Department of Labor, Bureau of Labor Statistics, "Databases, Tables & Calculators by Subject: Labor Force Statistics from the Current Population Survey," January 11, 2018, http://tinyurl.com/zyq5xlx.

13. Steve Eder, "Donald Trump Agrees to Pay $25 Million in Trump University Settlement," *New York Times,* November 18, 2016, http://tinyurl.com/h6eqcq2.

14. Sarah Carr, "Tomorrow's Test," *Slate,* June 5, 2016, http://tinyurl.com/hwnr9vo.

15. Ruth Marcus, "Welcome to the Post-Truth Presidency," *Washington Post,* December 2, 2016, http://tinyurl.com/jrbd4gd.

16. *Wikipedia, The Free Encyclopedia,* s.v. "Sundown Town" (accessed January 11, 2018), http://tinyurl.com/q64z9t5.

17. Janell Ross, "From Mexican Rapists to Bad Hombres, the Trump Campaign in Two Moments," *Washington Post,* October 20, 2016, http://tinyurl.com/m3af2p2.

18. Monica Davey, "He's a Local Pillar in a Trump Town. Now He Could Be Deported," *New York Times,* February 27, 2017, http://tinyurl.com/jrz5eoc.

19. Frank Pallotta, "Jon Stewart on Trump: 'We Have Never Faced This Before,'" *CNN Money,* February 1, 2017, http://tinyurl.com/ky9y78h.

20. Ira Glass, "The Beginning of Now: Act II—Who Tells Your Story?" *This American Life,* April 28, 2017, http://tinyurl.com/k3d6bdt.

21. Noor Wazwaz, "It's Official: The U.S. Is Becoming a Minority-Majority Nation," *U.S. News & World Report,* July 6, 2015, http://tinyurl.com/mtdpymf.

22. William Wordsworth, "The world is too much with us; late and soon," Bartleby.com, http://tinyurl.com/yv5eaf.

23. Thomas Merton, *Conjectures of a Guilty Bystander* (New York: Doubleday, 1966), 81.

24. The Congressional Civil Rights Pilgrimage is an annual event sponsored by the Faith & Politics Institute, http://tinyurl.com/y9wa7ct4.

25. "Selma, Alabama, (Bloody Sunday, March 7, 1965)," BlackPast.org, http://tinyurl.com/pwo7snb.

26. National Park Service, US Department of the Interior, "Brown Chapel AME Church," http://tinyurl.com/h5nu4ws.

VI. Keep Reaching In: Staying Engaged with Your Soul

1. "Du siehst, ich will viel .../You see, I want a ..." by Rainer Maria Rilke; from *Rilke's Book of Hours: Love Poems to*

God by Rainer Maria Rilke, translated by Anita Barrows and Joanna Macy, translation copyright © 1996 by Anita Barrows and Joanna Macy. Used by permission of Riverhead, an imprint of Penguin Publishing Group, a division of the Penguin Random House LLC, and the translators. All rights reserved.

2. Stanley Kunitz, "The Layers," in *Passing Through: The Later Poems, New and Selected* (New York: Norton, 1997), 107.

3. Annie Dillard, *Teaching a Stone to Talk* (New York: Harper & Row, 1982), 94–95.

4. "The Guest House" by Jalal al-Din Rumi and Coleman Barks (Trans.), from *The Essential Rumi* (New York: HarperOne, 2004). Reprinted with permission from the translator, Coleman Barks.

5. J. D. McClatchy, *Sweet Theft: A Poet's Commonplace Book* (Berkeley, CA: Counterpoint Press, 2016), 51.

6. Mohandas K. Gandhi, *Gandhi: An Autobiography—The Story of My Experiments with Truth* (Boston: Beacon Press, 1993).

7. Thomas Merton, *The Asian Journal of Thomas Merton* (New York: New Directions, 1973).

8. John Howard Griffin, *Follow the Ecstasy: The Hermitage Years of Thomas Merton* (San Antonio, TX: Wings Press, 2010).

9. John Middleton Murry, quoted in M. C. Richards, *Centering* (Middleton, CT: Wesleyan University Press, 1989), epigraph.

10. Thomas Merton, *Conjectures of a Guilty Bystander* (New York: Image, 1968), 153–154.

11. Nelle Morton, *The Journey Is Home*; "Nelle Katherine Morton Facts."

12. Howard Thurman, *The Inward Journey* (Richmond, IN: Friends United Press, 2007), 77.

13. Paul Tillich, *The Shaking of the Foundations* (Eugene, OR: Wipf & Stock, 2012), 155.

14. For more information about Valarie Kaur and her work, see http://valariekaur.com.

15. Georgia Keohane, "MLK, Civil Rights and the Fierce Urgency of Now," *Time,* January 19, 2015, http://tinyurl.com/y75ez78c.

16. To sign the declaration and for more information about the Revolutionary Love Project, see http://www.revolutionarylove.net/.

17. I was told this Hasidic tale by the philosopher Jacob Needleman, who kindly put it in writing for me so that I could recount it correctly.

18. *Wikipedia, The Free Encyclopedia,* s.v. "ORB Survey of Iraq War Casualties" (accessed January 11, 2018), http://tinyurl.com/pqdrz85.

19. *Wikipedia, The Free Encyclopedia,* s.v. "Casualties of the Iraq War" (accessed January 11, 2018), http://tinyurl.com/77g7ave.

20. There is much more on this topic in my book *Healing the Heart of Democracy: The Courage to Create a Politics Worthy of the Human Spirit* (San Francisco: Jossey-Bass, 2011 and 2014).

21. William Sloane Coffin, "Despair Is Not an Option," *The Nation,* January 12, 2004, http://tinyurl.com/ya5fnsuo.

22. "Lead" from *New and Selected Poems* by Mary Oliver. Published by Beacon Press, Boston. Copyright © 2005 by Mary Oliver. Reprinted by permission of The Charlotte Sheedy Literary Agency Inc.

23. "Autumn" from *Selected Poems of Rainer Maria Rilke,* a Translation from the German and Commentary by Robert Bly. Copyright © 1981 by Robert Bly. Reprinted with permission from HarperCollins Publishers.

24. Thomas Merton, "Hagia Sophia," in *A Thomas Merton Reader,* ed. Thomas P. McDonnell (New York: Doubleday, 1989), 506.

VII. Over the Edge: Where We Go When We Die

1. *Wikipedia, The Free Encyclopedia,* s.v. "Rule of Saint Benedict" (accessed November 3, 2017), http://tinyurl.com/b5t9dws.

2. *Wikipedia, The Free Encyclopedia,* s.v. "Order of Saint Benedict" (accessed December 16, 2017), http://tinyurl.com /y8pxwqtf.

3. *The Rule of Benedict,* Order of Saint Benedict, http://tinyurl .com/ycweregk.

4. Brother David Steindl-Rast, "Learning to Die," *Parabola* 2, no. 1 (Winter, 1977), http://tinyurl.com/ yclmyc9q.

5. Florida Scott-Maxwell, *The Measure of My Days* (New York: Penguin Books, 1983), 42.

6. Erik Erikson, *Childhood and Society* (New York: Norton, 1986).

7. e. e. cummings, "i thank You God for most this amazing," in *Selected Poems* (New York: Liveright, 2007), 167.

8. For information on the July 4 derecho, see "July 4–5, 1999 Derecho: 'The Boundary Waters—Canadian Derecho,'" http://tinyurl.com/5jefal.

9. *Wikipedia, The Free Encyclopedia,* s.v. "Julian of Norwich" (accessed Nov. 9, 2017), http://tinyurl.com/ya8esqa7.

About the Author

Parker J. Palmer is a writer, speaker, and activist who focuses on issues in education, community, leadership, spirituality, and social change. He is the founder and senior partner emeritus of the Center for Courage & Renewal. Palmer holds a PhD in sociology from the University of California, Berkeley, as well as thirteen honorary doctorates,  Photo by Sharon L. Palmer, September 2017. two Distinguished Achievement Awards from the National Educational Press Association, and an Award of Excellence from the Associated Church Press.

Palmer is the author of nine books—including several award-winning titles—that have sold over 1.5 million copies and been translated into twelve languages: *Healing the Heart of Democracy, The Courage to Teach, A Hidden Wholeness, Let Your Life Speak, The Active Life, To Know as We Are Known, The Company of Strangers, The Promise of*

Paradox, and *The Heart of Higher Education* (with Arthur Zajonc).

In 1998, the Leadership Project, a national survey of ten thousand educators, named Palmer one of the thirty "most influential senior leaders" in higher education and one of the ten key "agenda-setters" of the past decade. Since 2002, the Accrediting Commission for Graduate Medical Education has given annual Parker J. Palmer "Courage to Teach" and "Courage to Lead" Awards to directors of exemplary medical residency programs. In 2005, *Living the Questions: Essays Inspired by the Work and Life of Parker J. Palmer,* was published.

In 2010, Palmer was given the William Rainey Harper Award, whose previous recipients include Margaret Mead, Elie Wiesel, Marshall McLuhan, and Paolo Freire. In 2011, the Utne Reader named him one of twenty-five Visionaries on its annual list of "People Who Are Changing the World." In 2017, the Shalem Institute gave Palmer its annual Contemplative Voices Award, "created to honor those individuals who have made significant contributions to contemplative understanding, living and leadership and whose witness helps others live from the divine wellspring of compassion, strength, and authentic vision."

A member of the Religious Society of Friends (Quakers), Palmer lives in Madison, Wisconsin, with his wife, Sharon L. Palmer.

Berrett–Koehler
Publishers

Berrett-Koehler is an independent publisher dedicated to an ambitious mission: *Connecting people and ideas to create a world that works for all.*

We believe that the solutions to the world's problems will come from all of us, working at all levels: in our organizations, in our society, and in our own lives. Our BK Business books help people make their organizations more humane, democratic, diverse, and effective (we don't think there's any contradiction there). Our BK Currents books offer pathways to creating a more just, equitable, and sustainable society. Our BK Life books help people create positive change in their lives and align their personal practices with their aspirations for a better world.

All of our books are designed to bring people seeking positive change together around the ideas that empower them to see and shape the world in a new way.

And we strive to practice what we preach. At the core of our approach is Stewardship, a deep sense of responsibility to administer the company for the benefit of all of our stakeholder groups including authors, customers, employees, investors, service providers, and the communities and environment around us. Everything we do is built around this and our other key values of quality, partnership, inclusion, and sustainability.

This is why we are both a B-Corporation and a California Benefit Corporation—a certification and a for-profit legal status that require us to adhere to the highest standards for corporate, social, and environmental performance.

We are grateful to our readers, authors, and other friends of the company who consider themselves to be part of the BK Community. We hope that you, too, will join us in our mission.

A BK Life Book

BK Life books help people clarify and align their values, aspirations, and actions. Whether you want to manage your time more effectively or uncover your true purpose, these books are designed to instigate infectious positive change that starts with you. Make your mark!

To find out more, visit **www.bkconnection.com**.

Berrett–Koehler
Publishers

Connecting people and ideas
to create a world that works for all

Dear Reader,

Thank you for picking up this book and joining our world-wide community of Berrett-Koehler readers. We share ideas that bring positive change into people's lives, organizations, and society.

To welcome you, we'd like to offer you a free e-book. You can pick from among twelve of our bestselling books by entering the promotional code **BKP92E** here: http://www.bkconnection.com/welcome.

When you claim your free e-book, we'll also send you a copy of our e-newsletter, the *BK Communiqué*. Although you're free to unsubscribe, there are many benefits to sticking around. In every issue of our newsletter you'll find

- A free e-book
- Tips from famous authors
- Discounts on spotlight titles
- Hilarious insider publishing news
- A chance to win a prize for answering a riddle

Best of all, our readers tell us, "Your newsletter is the only one I actually read." So claim your gift today, and please stay in touch!

Sincerely,

Charlotte Ashlock
Steward of the BK Website

Questions? Comments? Contact me at bkcommunity@bkpub.com.

MIX
Paper from
responsible sources
FSC® C002589
www.fsc.org

Certified

Corporation
bcorporation.net